City Sidebar
The Book

Cara Curtin -
City Sidebar - The Book / Cara Curtin

www.caracurtin.com

Library of Congress Control Number: 2010939954
ISBN13: 978-0-9831094-0-2

Published by WordWorks Publishing
1417 Sadler Road #134
Fernandina Beach, FL 32034

Printed in the United States

Text Editing by Emily W. Carmain - www.noteworthyediting.com
Text Layout and Cover Design by Caroline Blochlinger - www.cbAdvertising.com

Reprinted by permission of:
The *News-Leader*, Fernandina Beach, Florida

City Sidebar

The Book

An irreverent look at life in Paradise

Cara Curtin

Acknowledgement

A special thank you goes to Publisher Foy Maloy and Michael Parnell, Editor, of the *News-Leader* for their support and encouragement.

Table of Contents

INTRODUCTION

THE PERILS OF PAULINE

THE VAGARIES OF LIFE

Table of Contents <small>(cont.)</small>

INTRODUCTION

Nobody reads introductions,
so I'll keep this short ...

This is All Foy Maloy's Fault

City Sidebar would never have happened without Foy Maloy and his bright ideas. It was 2001 and we were feverishly working to put the advertising campaign together for first Book Island Festival, destined to be renamed the Amelia Island Book Festival. The two of us, aided and abetted by the late Trudy Beckett, created, produced, and released a slick, multimedia campaign that reached the entire Southeast.

When the festival was over, I embarked on a well-deserved bit of relaxation by accompanying a friend on her drive out to Iowa and back. I got more than I bargained for on this trip, as you are about to learn.

I wrote the following article because I couldn't allow this amazing day of my vacation to fade away from memory. I gave it to Foy, mainly because I didn't know what else to do with it. He and the editor decided to run the piece in the *News-Leader*, and it apparently received good reviews.

Foy called. "We have to talk," he said, and *City Sidebar* was up and running.

Enjoy!
Cara

From False Alarms to Fried Chicken in Bed: Odysseys from the Road

We timed it just right. It was my birthday, and I was celebrating at the Flagship, the revolving restaurant atop one of the twin towers of the Galt House in Louisville, Kentucky. The city looked beautiful from 25 stories up, our dinner was delicious, and the nightcap in the bar was a perfect ending to the day.

Cindy Glenn and I had postponed our annual Fatathon until October of that year, and the fall colors on our first few days out of Fernandina Beach had been a just reward for our delayed departure. Tomorrow we would end our trek to Iowa and her cabin in the woods.

We finished our Bailey's Irish Cream and took the elevator down to our room on the 19th floor; we had asked to be put up high with a view of the Ohio River, and the clerk had readily complied. We enjoyed a last peek at the nightscape and repaired to our respective beds. Tomorrow we faced a nine-hour drive.

The alarm went off all too soon. Cindy was up and moving, but was making no effort to squelch the annoying beep. I headed for the clock radio and was shocked to discover it was only 4:30 am; surely some previous tenant had played a joke on us.

"Get dressed," Cindy said. "Now. It's a fire alarm."

I reversed direction and threw on a sweatshirt over my filmy nightclothes. The nights were still warm enough for me to have left my coat in the car 19 stories below us. Sweatshirt, tennis shoes, and nightgown didn't qualify me for America's best-dressed, but that competition wasn't high on my priorities at the moment.

I followed Cindy out our door and down the hall. No one joined us, and I was afraid we'd be the only disheveled women in nightclothes when we reached the lobby. We began to pick up fellow travelers as we went down flight after flight of stairs, and I was somewhat mollified to see that they looked no better than we did. Our small gaggle was still three stories up when the stairwell ended; rather than wandering our way through strange hallways, Cindy and I led our party through the fire doors on our left. (I had always wanted to push through a door marked FIRE DOOR; ALARM WILL SOUND, but now I was too sleepy and in too much of a hurry to enjoy it.)

Unfortunately, this door led to a deck with no apparent exit. Now someone else took the lead, and we soon landed in the lobby of the tower opposite ours. From there, we sat in relative comfort and watched as fire, police, and hotel management handled the problem. Someone finally turned off the alarm, and my ears stopped ringing. Just as I began to grumble that they could have at least provided us with coffee while we watched, we were given the signal to resume our normal lives. The few staff members we encountered on our way back to the 19th floor of our own tower could offer no explanation of what had happened, but the tow truck driver explained it all later that day. (Stay tuned.)

We were back in our room by 5:30. "Ya know, if we clean up now and have breakfast, we'll get an early start on that nine-hour drive," I offered.

"And we'd get to the cabin in daylight, instead of fumbling around in the dark, like we usually do," Cindy agreed.

We were clean and dressed, fed, and packed by 7:30. Cindy retrieved the Volvo from the garage while I handled luggage and the bell person. We loaded the car and paid the bill. Cindy turned the ignition key, and— nothing. The lights came on, but the engine didn't.

AAA promised a jump/tow within 45 minutes. Cindy went to find us more coffee while I called the local Volvo dealer to warn the service department that we would be dropping by. The owner of Bottom Line Towing showed up in 30 minutes, bless his heart.

During our trip across Louisville (Have you ever noticed that when your car is dead, help is always miles away?) the driver explained that a friend of his worked at the Galt House; they'd been having problems with a self-activating fire alarm system. "Great," I grumbled, "I really enjoyed running around the hotel in my nightgown."

We exhausted that topic fairly quickly, so the driver brought up his favorite subject: women with car problems. This recitation quickly deteriorated into women in general, closely followed by his all-time favorite topic, his ex-wife. He proudly proclaimed he could still feel the satisfying *smack* of his fist colliding with her boyfriend's mouth. Six months in jail had been time will spent.

We were at Tafel Volvo by 10 a.m. The service representative assured us we'd be on our way well before lunch.

Cindy and I walked down to Pizza Hut at 1:30, right after the service rep gently explained that my car's gear position switch had eaten itself. (That's the hoochie that tells your automatic transmission that it's in Park, so it's OK to start the engine.)

While that problem was relatively quick and easy to fix, the bolt that had sheared off during this repair work was not. After the mechanic had lunch, he would drill out the sheared bolt, and then insert a threaded sleeve to accept a new one.

The pizza and beer did their trick, and our nap in the waiting room compensated us a little for the 4:30 a.m. reveille. The service rep woke us with the bill in his hand.

We were on the road again by 3:30, but knew that Iowa was out of the question that day. We decided to drive for as long as we could, then find an inexpensive (and unbudgeted) place to stay. Cindy drove while I researched the AAA Tour Book for the likely spots to stop.

We made it to Danville, Illinois. It's halfway between Louisville and the Champagne-Urbana area, if that means anything to you.

The young woman at the Days Inn gave us each a bright smile and a large bottle of water. The only water I wanted at that point was to be mixed with my scotch.

"What's this for?" I asked.

"We've had so much rain lately that the city water system is messed up; we're under a Boil Order."

"Is the bar open? Does it have ice?" We peppered her with questions. Yes and yes. The day was not a total disaster.

The first glass of therapy disappeared quickly. We regaled each other, and then finally the other bar patrons, with tidbits from our day: the fire drill, the combative tow truck driver, gear position sensors, and sheared bolts. Halfway through my second scotch, I fervently declared that all I wanted was quick dinner and a long snooze. "How late is the dining room open?"

"Oh, the kitchen's closed; water's been turned off at the main," the bartender explained. Cindy and I dissolved into hysterical laughter and ordered another drink.

I can honestly say that, before that night, I had never eaten KFC in bed in my jammies. At least we were on the first floor; I wouldn't have to climb down another nineteen floors if the fire alarm went off.

1 February 2002

THE PERILS OF PAULINE

Coffee That's Not Good 'til the Last Drop

I have named our new, whiz-bang coffeemaker HAL, in honor of the deranged computer in *2001: Space Odyssey*.

"Good morning, HAL."

"Good morning, Dr. Chandra. I have made the coffee."

"This coffee is very good, HAL, but it is cold."

"Yes, isn't that wonderful? I have been programmed to turn myself off after I have been on for what my maker has deemed an appropriate amount of time."

"No, that is not wonderful. I want you to turn on and off at my convenience, and not at some arbitrary time determined by a lab rat."

With that, I marched myself to the telephone to call the Mr. Coffee customer service number, 1-800-IGNORE. I punched my way through an overly complicated menu until a metallic voice warned me that my wait to talk to a warm body could very well exceed five minutes.

I read a page and a half of the funnies—as well as Annie's Mailbox and the Super Quiz—before Ms. Perky identified herself at Kelly. Our conversation careered rapidly downhill as she deteriorated from bright and bubbly to frigidly polite. She, like HAL, was inordinately proud that he could and would deactivate himself without any human intervention.

"But what," I asked, "am I to do if I want a hot cup of coffee three or four hours after the brew cycle?"

I developed a slight tic in one eye as she lectured me about how coffee that's four hours old needs to be poured down the drain. After more overly-polite conversation, I ascertained that there was no way I could end-run the two-hour cutoff. Kelly was stunned when I told her that I found this infernal machine to be unsatisfactory, and was going to replace it with another brand that would do what I wanted it to.

It was only after Kelly and I had ended our short and unpleasant relationship that I realized I couldn't even give HAL to charity; I didn't want to inflict his poor engineering on people I didn't know and who'd never done anything to deserve such ill treatment from me.

My Adult Supervision and I have spent the ensuing weeks trying to outsmart a mere coffeemaker, and I am embarrassed to admit that we don't always win. Whoever sleeps in a little later runs the risk of getting a lukewarm reception from HAL. I have found that I take great glee in turning him off just before his cutoff time, and then turning him right back on. That usually starts HAL's countdown program all over again, but not always. The mornings that this ploy does work, I am ashamed to admit, I do a little jig—Yess!—in my kitchen.

After knowing HAL this short period of time, I think I now understand why my iron turns herself off and sputters all over the shirt I'm almost finished ironing. She, like HAL, has this wonderful safety cutoff feature that manages to make using our modern conveniences more frustrating and difficult.

This over-concern with our safety—and the not-too-subtle message that we're too stupid to see to it ourselves—is not limited to small appliances. I have several friends whose automobiles decide when to lock and unlock their doors. What if our wishes don't coincide with our cars' programming? What if you want to keep your doors locked after you turn off the engine? And the idea of driving down the Interstate with my doors locked scares me to death; how will the EMTs get to me if have a heart attack or am injured in an accident? Or have the geniuses in the auto industry designed these doors to unlock on impact? So far, my Volvos have been immune to this insanity, but since Ford acquired Volvo, I figure it's only a matter of time before my car also has a mind of its own.

Haven't any of the designers of our appliances and autos ever read any of the science fiction out there that describes a world in which the machines are brighter and are in more control than the humans? It makes a great story, but I don't think much of the reality. And even more important, I really do not want to lose my ability to turn machines on and off at my convenience.

Having said all of that, I think I'll heat my cold coffee in the microwave and ask HAL if the clothes dryer will tell him what he has done with my favorite tee shirt.

6 May 2005

Riding the Information (Dirt) Road

I am convinced that one of the reasons I have the pleasure of writing for the *News-Leader* is that I once politely refused Foy Maloy's offer to give me his cell phone number.

Foy and I worked together on the publicity campaign for the first Book Island Festival. Since we were inventing it as we went along, life became pretty hectic and more than a mite intense for several months. During one of our last meetings before the inaugural event, I agreed to check on a loose end and call him with the results later that day. When Foy offered his cell phone number, I politely said, "No, thank you; I don't need it. If you're not in the office, I'll either leave a message or call you tomorrow."

There was a moment of stunned silence before he whooped with laughter. "Great! I like the way you do business!"

That exchange has given me pause to think about all of today's technology that I am (mostly) blissfully ignorant about, and not just a little hostile toward. Offhand, I cannot think of a single soul I want to talk to while I'm driving, nor do I need to bother someone else while they are similarly occupied. I cannot imagine anything I have to say that is important enough to interrupt someone else's meal, meeting, or quiet evening at home.

I do not need a Palm Pilot to schedule my trips to aerobics at the MacArthur YMCA or to Publix and Wal-Mart, and a BlackBerry is something you're supposed to put on your Cheerios, not carry around with you. Neither do I need a fax machine. I seriously doubt any of my book exchange customers will ever ask me to fax them a copy of *War and Peace*.

I must confess, however reluctantly, that I do own a computer, a model one of my more techno-literate acquaintenances has dubbed a dinosaur. I use it mostly as a word processor to produce neatly typed copy for Editor Michael Parnell.

I knew I was a stranger in the strange land of computers when I recently told someone that I wasn't on the Interstate. Her blank look told me I had misspoken, and it took me several embarrassed moments to explain why I have no desire to be on the Internet. I find it very telling that the people who race along that information highway regularly complain about spam, viruses, and interminable e-mails with multiple attachments. A first class stamp cleverly avoids these pitfalls.

If you are curling your lip at my illiteracy, I must remind you that the purpose of our blissful island lifestyle is to unplug and listen to the surf, to have our morning coffee on the deck at a civilized hour, and to do things as they fit into our own schedules, rather than someone else's.

If you call to tell me what an ostrich or dinosaur I am (take your pick), you will not be interrupted by those annoying beeps that signal that someone more important than you wants to talk to me. If I don't answer the telephone at all, you can't leave me a message, because I don't have Voice Mail.

I just have one final point to make: I drafted this column, as I do every column, in longhand, using my 20-year old Schaeffer fountain pen.

Eat bytes and die.

9 May 2003

It's About Time for This Disorder

Thank goodness, I have just discovered that I am not a ditz after all, but suffer from a little-known disorder. You may have noticed that sometimes there is an interruption in the smooth flow of these columns. That's because I have a timing disorder, according to Ellen Goodman's March 28th column. (Perhaps the first disorder we should address is that of procrastination—her column festered on my desk for a couple of months before I read it.)

My timing disorder manifests itself when I live two very event-filled weeks and call them one. While Ms Goodman did not specifically address my malady, I learned enough from her column to diagnose myself. My affliction is time compression; I compress the two weeks I've lived in Paradise to just seven days. It's not that hard to do; I arise early each day to ensure that I have enough time to squeeze all of the fun I have planned into the short 24 hours allotted to me. My calendar is filled with notations about lunch dates, receptions, book signings, and appointments.

I'm sure you've noticed that I have neglected to set aside a period for sleep. I don't have to schedule any downtime; it happens spontaneously. I run from one fun-filled event to another until I topple over, not unlike a giant redwood. When I wake up seven or eight hours later, my fun starts all over again.

What makes my case so interesting—at least to the supermarket tabloids—is that it is usually experienced by vacationers, the implication being that when we're on our own turf, we have a pretty good handle on our place in the whole space-time continuum thing. But once we stray from home base, we find ourselves arguing that today is Thursday, not Friday. While researchers agree that vacationtime decalibrates our internal calendar, they have failed to note that vacationers with a Saturday departure compress time. If this really is Friday, their departure is tomorrow, not the day after. They have one less day in Paradise than they thought.

I can't tell you how happy I am to discover my condition. It means that I have a disability, and therefore am not responsible for missed deadlines, appointments, or birthdays. I wonder if I qualify for special benefits or monetary compensation from a government agency. Am I now qualified to use a handicapped parking spot? Not only would I avoid the label of ditz, I might even be entitled to a government stipend.

Speaking of the government and its stipends, I wish my diagnosis had been tendered before I retired. As you can imagine, the Navy takes a dim view about the untimely executions of one's duties and assignments. And let's not even talk about missing a Thursday meeting because I was busy living through the second Wednesday of the week. Nor do I want to remember the year I added an extra April so I could have plenty of time to meet an important May deadline. Can you imagine me in charge of D-Day? We'd be commemorating it in July or August!

To return to Ms. Goodman and her discussion of time, she concentrated her column on time-bulimia. Time-bulimics stuff their schedules to bursting. Then, when reality dawns—along with the day from Heck that they've scheduled for themselves—they purge their calendars down to skin and bones. When they reschedule all of those commitments, they overstuff a day in their future, which they will have to purge when it comes around.

This over-scheduling of one's day is called "irrational exuberance." While I am not a time-bulimic, I am guilty of irrational exuberance about what I can accomplish in one day. Only someone afflicted with this exuberance would think that she could go for her morning walk before she does laundry, irons, cleans closets, goes grocery shopping, takes a nap, and is a charming and witty dinner companion. Painful experience has taught me to schedule only two of the above activities: a nap plus being charming and witty during dinner, preferably in a local restaurant's dining room.

My editor, bless his heart, no longer calls me to inquire politely about the status of my column, which is sometimes days overdue. I can only imagine the conversation at the *News-Leader* when my column is AWOL: "Cara's goofed up her schedule again; she'll hand in her column next week and wonder why we don't run it." What they don't realize is that I'm planning to write it the second Tuesday of next week.

27 May 2005

Navigation Proves Difficult for Some

I didn't know I had a problem until I started driving. When you start driving, I quickly discovered, people start giving you directions. "Go west six blocks on State Street, then turn north onto Glenn Avenue." Saywhat?

By the time the direction-giver had repeated himself several times, all semblances of courtesy and helpfulness had vanished. Clenched jaws and tight lips began to bark commands of where to turn and how far to drive.

Drawing a map and jabbing at the lines on paper didn't help, because my brain had shut down. Shut down, my fat fanny; my poor little brain had flat melted. By this time, two or three well-meaning people would be gathered around me, each jabbering incomprehensible directions.

After one particularly confusing and frustrating session, I politely looked at the loudest and most vociferous direction-giver and said, "So, does that mean I turn left when I leave the parking lot?"

It didn't take me long to develop a camouflage procedure whenever anyone attempted to tell me how to proceed from Point A to Point B. After only a couple of experiences where people ended up red faced and shouting, I knew I had to do something to protect both of us. And when one well-meaning friend loudly demanded, "What's wrong with you? Everybody knows that Wilson Boulevard runs east and west!" Well, no, they don't; I once spent an entire afternoon trying to get two parallel streets to meet in Orange Park. I was always too embarrassed to explain my deficiency to my exasperated companion, so I smiled sweetly, took the map, and started out on my journey.

Sometimes I'd get to Point B safely, only to spend my time there dreading the drive back home to Point A. I would usually get home safely, but every once in a while, no matter how carefully I turned the map upside down, I just couldn't figure out how to retrace my outward journey back to my point of origin.

That's why, during the process of discovering that I was navigationally challenged, I also discovered the wonderful world of panic attacks. My brain would sauté in its own juices and I would have to park the car until the tears and the shakes subsided. Then I'd repair my makeup and find a filling station attendant (remember those?) to help me find my way home. Ask my husband about the day I was to meet him at Mayport Naval Station and ended up in St Augustine.

I eventually developed coping techniques: "I'm so sorry I can't come to your house on Friday night; I have a conflict." Yeah, right. The only conflict I had was about following the map I'd been given. By that time, I was already a veteran of getting so hopelessly lost on my way to an event that I just gave up and went home. Sometimes, I'd been so lost that I had no idea how I fumbled my way home; familiar landmarks would appear magically and I could skitter back to my hidey hole. After

I'd calmed down, I'd begin to make up some lame excuse to my friends about my no-show.

The regulars at Brett's still laugh about the out-of-towners who arrived at this riverside establishment late one afternoon. The man made a great production of choosing just the right seats at the bar for him and his wife, accompanied by this explanation: "I've driven all day to get here so we can watch the sunset over the Gulf!"

Can you imagine what would have happened if he and I had married one another? We wouldn't have been able to find our way out of the church!

Speaking of spouses, my own dear Andrew is the only person who can give me directions I can follow. After an initial period of disbelief, he began to write out directions for me on index cards. I carried some of those cards in my wallet for years. We met in 1970, when I was stationed at Naval Air Station Pensacola and he was stationed at the nearby Naval Air Field Ellyson. The written directions for the 30-minute drive from my base to his remained taped to my glove box for the three years I lived in Pensacola.

When change of station orders had me driving from Pensacola to Newport, Rhode Island, Andy confessed to me much later that he and my secretary had placed bets on the odds of my ever being seen again.

Fortunately, Andrew has remained amused all of these years by my lack of direction. One of his endearments for me is "Prince Henry the Navigator." He used to tell me that he expected a panicked telephone call from his lost wife. He'd ask me where I was, and I would answer, "I'm in a telephone booth!" Only when he at last becomes exasperated with my deficiency does he call me

"Magellan." That's my clue to stop being myself and try to be someone whose compass isn't slightly off kilter.

I keep telling people that Amelia Island is paradise on earth, but not for the reasons that normal people have. One of the many reasons I think this island's so great— aside from the usuals of climate, people, recreation— is that God, in His infinite wisdom, has seen to it that I have retired to a small island and a small town that's laid out in a grid. (Thank you, Senator Yulee.) For the first time in my life, I can give and receive directions like everyone else.

Oh, I still end up in places I didn't intend to, but that's usually because I'm too busy composing deathless prose (or tonight's dinner) in my head to pay attention to the here and now. I work on Centre Street, which bisects the island from east (ocean) to west (river). Even I can keep that straight. And with just a little bit of work, I can tell you that something's on the northeast corner of Centre and a cross street, or that Fort Clinch is east of 8th. Prince Henry would be so proud of me!

1 August 2003

A Potpourri of Pet Peeves

I remember loudly announcing a few months ago that I was entering the winter season with a new attitude. If you read the fine print carefully, you will see that nowhere is the claim made that this new attitude would be a better one.

I have, therefore, spent the last two yukky months working up a list of favorite pet peeves. While I do not consider myself an overly demanding person, several phenomena of everyday life have become worth noting. I present them to you for both your edification and enjoyment.

Pet Peeve #1: Like any (credit) card-carrying true blue American, I took advantage of the post-holiday sales. My Adult Supervision muttered something about going broke saving money, but I did not let his negative attitude deter me from one of a girl's favorite pastimes. What brought me to a dead stop, however, was the realization that clothing manufacturers must think that chubby matrons have long arms. Each morning I eagerly donned yet another newly purchased top, and then stared at myself in the mirror in dismay. The sleeves ended several inches past my fingertips! I had to take each blouse, shirt, and jacket to Gwen Mullin at Just Sew to have several inches removed from the sleeves. (Gwen and her staff, by the way, are veritable magicians with a needle and thread. Should you ever need her services, you can find her at the 24 Hour Laundry Zone in the Eight Flags Shopping Center on 14th Street.)

The thought did occur to me that Garfield has been right all of these years: I am not overweight after all; I am merely undertall. If I were as tall as my weight indicates I should be, my arms would match my sleeve length. I hope my vertically challenged condition is addressed by the American Disabilities Act.

Pet Peeve #2: "Are these books in any order?" I have always wanted to answer that with, "No, madam; a dump truck backs up to the front door the first of every week." Of course, I'd never say that. The books are carefully catalogued and alphabetized, which I assure you are never-ending tasks. Don't tell anyone, but all of that orderliness is for my benefit, not the customers'. How can I sell a book if I can't find it? Every time a customer is amazed at my ability to pluck the right book off of the shelf, I just smile sweetly and oh, so gently, remove the money from his or her hand.

Pet Peeve #3: The talking head on Headline News announced the other day that 400,000 Americans die each year from obesity and its complications.

I have always hated being part of the crowd, and have spent the last several years trying to separate myself from the (overweight) masses. That's when I discovered that it's very difficult—if not downright impossible—to find exercise clothes for us "full figured" women. You'd think, wouldn't you, that there would be a … er … large selection of these bigger sizes; after all, who needs to exercise more?

After visiting every sports attire retailer in the vicinity, as well as several in Jacksonville, I have come to the conclusion that clothing manufacturers believe that only skinny people exercise. I also think that whoever assigns size numbers to this attire must be anorexic. Her idea of "XL" and my idea of "XL" are several inches apart. And of course, there's no 2X or 3X; they simply don't exist. I suspect that they're assuming that chubby people don't exercise. If the "War on Obesity" ever lurches off of the starting block, more and more oversized people are going to be looking for something to wear while they join the battle.

I've often said how impressed I am that the residents of this island come from such diverse backgrounds. If any of you have ties to the garment trade, please clip this pet peeve and deliver it to someone who recognizes the large (get it?) untapped market of exercise clothing for the supersized men and women in our midst.

Pet Peeve #4: It doesn't happen very often, thank heavens, but every once in a while, a customer will stop just inside my book shop door and say, "I don't suppose you have any idea what you have, do you?" I take a deep breath and allow propriety and greed to keep me from delivering the most satisfying reply of, "No, sir; I just sit here and look at picture books all day long."

As any retailer can tell you, I'd better have a good idea of what's on my shelves. How can I sell it if I don't know I have it? The many books in my inventory provide a never-ending occupation for even the most devout fussbudget. I can promise you that, more often than not, I can visualize—*in situ*, of course—the very tome you are in search of.

I assure you, Gentle Reader, that I am not a cranky person. My needs and expectations are very simple, really: I'd like to have clothes that fit both my body and my lifestyle; I'd like to have a gentle but witty riposte to customers' queries, and I'd really, really like to have a tasty, low-calorie, low-carb version of mashed potatoes.

26 March 2004

Numbers Are Not Our Friends

Jill has three apples and Donna has four. They want to combine them, and then give half of them to Slater. How many apples will Slater receive? Even as a little kid, I knew the answer to this one: Who cares? Let Slater buy his own apples.

My Dad, bless his heart, is a structural engineer, and he and his math skills have provided for his family quite nicely, thank you. Long before computers and CADs, my dad used yellow paper, a graphite holder, and a pearl eraser to compute and draft the exact dimensions of bridges and the steel skeletons of buildings. Years later he worked at home, and I discovered that he was a mumbler. He'd converted the garage into a drawing room (literally), and would stand out there and figure and mumble and draw and mumble all day long. Our big red Persian cat was his constant companion, and every once in a while she would make her own raspy contribution to the process. But no matter how hard he tried all of these years, he's never understood how and why his only chick could be so baffled by numbers.

Numbers, I learned at a very early age, are not our friends. My parents conspired with my teachers to disabuse me of this prejudice, but to no avail. Numbers are the reason I dislike oatmeal to this day. My teacher would assign me extra arithmetic homework, and my dad would help me with it, but only after all of my other work was completed. (Oh, yippee; what an incentive to finish early!)

I found multiplication tables especially baffling, and Dad would put me through multiplication drills until my eyes glazed over. Over our bowls of oatmeal the next morning, he'd ask me how much nine times seven was, and would get no response. He'd finally look over at me, and my tears would be dripping into my oatmeal. Poor little kid, I'd forgotten everything he'd drilled me on the night before. I still don't know my ninezies; that's why we invented calculators. If my calculator dies, I will have to close my shop so I can go buy a new one.

I inherited my math skills—or a lack thereof—from the maternal side of the house. Mom would periodically call Dad while he was at work to ask what one half of 2/3 of a cup was. She was obviously halving a recipe for dinner, and had not yet discovered the secret I unearthed years later, when I started messing up my own kitchen. One simply fixes the recipe as directed, and then freezes the leftovers in meal-size portions. Just be sure you really like Tuna Surprise before you fix it, because the six that the "serves six" at the bottom of the recipe refers to clearly means six Jaguar linebackers after a hard day of practice.

Having more or less mastered grammar school arithmetic, I was deemed ready to enter the wonderful world of mathematics. Good thing I wasn't given a vote; if I'd had my way, I'd still be blissfully unaware of the very existence—never mind the purpose—of quadratic equations. Now that I am all grown up, I have relegated them to the same rubbish bin in which I stuffed pluperfect endings for Latin verbs.

To this day, I contend that algebra is an exercise in self-abuse; never once have I had the necessity as an adult to know what X squared plus Y squared is equal to. There are no Xs or Ys on my bank statement, and, come to think of it, there aren't any in my cookbooks, either. Since it's tax time, I should point out that the Feds don't ask for X amount—they merely want it all. Algebra gives letters a bad name; X and Y should sue for damages.

But God is not totally unkind to those of us who are numerically challenged. While I love words and roll them around my tongue like aged beef or brandy, my father doesn't know alliteration from apples. Speaking of apples, I wonder if Slater would give me half of his half of the apples that Jill and Donna gave him. Just how many apples is that?

8 April 2005

Some Weeks Need Eight Days

If this week doesn't have eight days in it, I'm dead meat. This is Friday, but my food diary tells me I have eaten my way to breakfast on Sunday.

"Weight control" has become my least favorite oxymoron. My most recent experiences while trying to reduce the amount of space I take up sound more like one-liners from your favorite stand-up comic. I can almost hear the rim shot, even as we speak.

A friend advised me to reduce or remove the white foods from my diet: bread, potatoes, rice. After some discussion about the matter, we decided to reduce the white and go with wheat. My Adult Supervision lost 10 pounds. I gained at least five. (*Badda-bing.*) After a long heart-felt conversation with my doctor, plus a few tears, he prescribed an appetite suppressant. My weigh-in a month later showed that I had gained more weight. (*Badda-bam.*) After contributing four tubes of blood to a local laboratory, I was told the good news: all of my metabolic regulators are operating normally. And then there was the bad news: my metabolic system is operating normally. (*Badda-bong.*) There's more good news: I'm only eating about 1,100-1,200 calories a day, and my log shows I'm exercising about 15 days out of 30. (*Badda-boom*.) And more bad news: My sore Australian hip is so unhappy with this regimen that I'm back on the injured/reserve list. (*Badda-bang*.)

When I was a 98-pound weakling, I complained about how hard it was to find anything small enough to wear. Now I have the opposite problem. Have you ever been in a "plus" size shop? It's quite an education. Judging by some of the disasters I see hanging on the rack, I do believe someone in the industry hates us larger-than-life women and wants us to look as big as a barn and twice as ugly. The design that is guaranteed to make me foam at the mouth is the Middy style blouse, with a wide, horizontal band as its hem. Sometimes, this band is in a contrasting color and does wonders to accentuate what is often the widest portion of our anatomy. I don't mind looking a little zaftig, but this is ridiculous.

And you can forget about the nicer shops with all of those wonderful status labels; most of these oh-so-trendy designers do not extend their lines that far up the size chart. Stylish and chubby cannot be seen in the same sentence. As I carefully explained to one of our clothing retailers the other day, there are a lot of chubby women on this island, and some of us have the money to spend building a fashionable wardrobe. Her eyes glazed over, but she said she'd pass that information along to management. Fat chance (you should pardon the expression); she's never been bigger than a size 7, and obviously hasn't a clue about how frustrating it is to be overweight and want to look sharp at the same time.

Speaking of frustration, I finally understand why some young women become bulimic or anorexic. It's tough denying yourself the yummies that everyone else is scarfing down. One of my friends offered me some of her coconut cake from K.P.'s the other day, and it killed me to limit myself to one forkful. I have admired K.P.'s bakery goods from afar for years. If I'm ever on death row, my last meal is going to be one of their desserts AND the Decadent Brownie (with extra chocolate sauce) from Brett's Waterway Café. What do I care if my survivors have to pay for an extra-wide coffin?

I also understand why there are so many weight loss programs, diet plans, exercise regimens and machines—not to mention funky pills, drinks, and unguents—all guaranteed to make the fat magically disappear. And let's not forget the scary surgical procedures that desperate people purchase. Lucky for the rest of us, I think your pocketbook has to be as large as your hips before you can partake of some of these options.

Lest you think that I am the only cranky weight-challenged matron on the island, let me assure you that I have talked to a fair number of women who are approximately my size and my age. Their reaction to this (possibly) age-related weight problem is as varied as their hair color. Some women are at peace with themselves and their size, sort of: This is the size I am and the size I'm going to be; get used to it. Some women are deep into, if not self-hate, at least self-blame: If I'd stop eating, I'd lose a couple of dress sizes. And then there's the third group I've found. We haven't given up and accepted our current size, but we're not mad at ourselves, either. But we are convinced that somewhere in this world there's the magic combination of diet, exercise, and modern metabolic science that will help us beat this thing down a couple of dress sizes.

Until that happens, you'll find me in the gym or at the salad bar; just don't stand between me and the tomato wedges.

5 November 2004

Trouble Always Comes in Threes

I was busy chasing after a Cheerio in a puddle of milk the other morning in Paradise, when our television said, "Urk," and died. I knew it was dead, because it smelled funny.

We all know that trouble comes in threes, but I had no idea that the death of our television would merely be the opening act of the stereotypical terrible trio.

I tried not to get too upset at the dead TV, because we'd been expecting it for some time. Andy and I can't agree when we brought it home, but it was at least 15 long, hard years ago, and the guys at Fernandina Television Repair on 8th Street have told us not to bring it in again. I guess they'd had to whittle new parts for it after it got hit by lightning the second time. (Whoever said "lightning never strikes the same spot twice" never owned a piece of expensive electronic equipment in Florida.)

The death of the television came at a particularly inconvenient time for the Curtins. Andy and I had just sat down and carefully choreographed the next six weeks. It was going to be a complicated tap dance, but we'd make it, if no one tripped or stumbled. When the TV tripped, stumbled, and then fell in a heap, we were not only out a TV, but also out of time and opportunity to replace it. I made a point not to complain; after all, one of my book shop's mottoes is "Kill Your Television."

Our next carefully choreographed step was Andy's week-long trip to Mobile, Alabama. I always enjoy his trips, because they give me the opportunity to delve into projects best executed with no adult supervision. I also take this opportunity to dine on gourmet fare that makes my husband retch, like liverwurst and sauerkraut—but not in the same meal, I can assure you.

I was two days into my solo act when I climbed into the shower after my morning walk, only to discover I had no water. Since I was definitely deficient in the sugar and spice department, my waterless state was a major problem. I called Karl Weilbacher, Jr, Plumbing, and soon his son Chris was giving me a lesson in Water Softener 101. Fortunately, the Weilbachers are not only expert plumbers, but are also fans of Labrador retrievers; Chris did not seem to mind the help our Lab was determined to provide. We both agreed that most things work better with a little puppy snort on them, anyway.

Andy returned from Mobile on Thursday. The TV was still broken, the water softener had died, but we had running water. We looked at each other over the pork chops Thursday night: Two down, one to go.

The next morning we began to pack for our next act of choreography: Andy would fly us to Memphis, Tennessee, to party with old friends. Friday morning grew warmer and warmer while we packed for our fun-filled weekend. By the time we were ready for our showers, the house had grown quite stuffy. It was the perfect opportunity to launch the central air conditioning on its inaugural voyage for the season.

The A/C had other ideas. We quickly realized that if nothing happens when you punch "Cool" for the function and "Auto" for the fan, the next button you have to punch is the telephone number for the repairman.

We agreed that this third catastrophe would be the end of our troubles and took our showers without benefit of cool air. The only glitch in that plan was the dribble of water coming out of Andy's shower head.

We finally took off for Memphis, clean and packed, with Watson Electric scheduled to look at the air conditioner and Chris Weilbacher scheduled for a return visit on Monday after our weekend of partying.

We awoke Saturday morning to discover that our troubles were not yet over. I had just stepped out of the shower in the Memphis motel, when Andy quietly announced that we were going home. Bad weather was coming our way, and it was either leave Saturday morning or stay in this motel until Tuesday while the weather dumped inches of rain on our head.

I suggested Saturday night in Savannah (another favorite city) instead of Fernandina Beach. "Yes," Andy said. "Why go home? We have no TV, no water softener, no air conditioning, and my shower just drools."

So the Curtins, like grasshoppers instead of ants, flew to Savannah and had a lovely dinner, plus beignets at Huey's the next morning, before we flew home to be grown-ups again.

29 April 2004

THE VAGARIES OF LIFE

Age and I.Q. Clash

I always said that when my age and my IQ grew to be the same number, I'd quit counting birthdays. Those two numbers collided last week, and I can assure you that it was not a pretty sight. As with any milestone birthday, mine started me thinking about the ageing process in general and my own in particular.

I went to one of those touchy-feely workshops several years ago, and the facilitator posed this question: You obviously know your chronological age, but whenever you think of yourself, what age are you? That exercise made me realize that I thought of myself as 35, regardless of my true age. Thirty-five meant that I'd been working long enough to know what I was doing; I was earning a sufficient amount of money; and I was still young and healthy enough to enjoy my labor and the fruits thereof.

The birthday last week made me realize that I still think of myself as 35, despite the passing years. But 35-year-olds usually don't have arthritis or need a mid-day nap. Nor do they have a pill caddy to tell them what day of the week it is.

I knew I was getting older when someone told me that Beyonce is not a fabric softener and Eminem is not a candy that melts in my mouth instead of in my hand.

My first Geritol moment came when I discovered a book about Woodstock in the history section, and things have been going downhill since then. I stopped listening to the oldies station when I realized that I had heard all of those songs when they were first released—and had danced to them in a classmate's new-fangled architectural invention called a rumpus room. My newest Geritol moment came when someone asked me, not if I had children, but if I had grandchildren!

I'm so old I remember when all of the other girls got Princess telephones in their bedrooms. Not me, though; my father said the plain black one on the kitchen wall worked just fine, thank you. It's not surprising, then, that I own no cell phone that's plastered to my ear. Who are all of these people talking to, anyway, and what on earth are they talking about? Do I really want to know?

And I remember Dad refusing to buy our first television set until they came down in price. He was right; two or three years after everyone else in the neighborhood had one, our much cheaper set arrived. That delivery led to my infatuation with the characters my dad referred to as Gene Artery, Lope-Along Cassidy, and the Crisco Kid. To this day, I announce my readiness to depart the scene by announcing, "Hey, Cisco! Let's went!" (That was the running gag of Pancho, the chubby sidekick of "The Cisco Kid.")

One of the larger mistakes I've made in the aging process is trying to explain to today's college students that at my college, freshmen girls weren't allowed to talk to boys after 7 p.m. during the week. (I know that's true, because I broke the rule and was denied the privilege of talking to any boys at all for one very long and silent week.)

I was long out of saddle shoes and poodle skirts when we slapped bar codes on everything, and I distinctly remember announcing that pantyhose were a dumb idea. What woman would throw away a perfectly good leg of hosiery just because the other one bit the dust?

I knew I was old when the car salesman couldn't understand why anyone would want to drive a stick shift. I left him standing in his showroom when he said he doubted that his mechanic could work on a clutch. And let's not even talk about the day the more mature manager had to drive my car through the full service car wash because none of his younger subordinates knew how to shift!

I knew I'd reached full cootdom when I remembered that I used to look at younger people and feel square because I wasn't keeping up with the latest fashions, dance steps, and jargon. Now I just feel offended at the amount of skin they display, the way they wiggle their tight young bodies on the dance floor, and their extremely limited vocabulary.

I always said that when I got to be of a Certain Age, I'd stop worrying about how bad I am at remembering names. I'd just call everyone Sweetie and be done with it. Well, I hope you liked this column, Sweetie, because that day is here.

31 October 2003

Be Careful What You Wish For

Back when we were wise high school seniors, my girlfriends and I whiled away one long afternoon with the philosophical discussion about what three wishes we would ask of the Genie in the Bottle.

Dad moved us across the state shortly after graduation, and I lost touch with all of those young girls. I like to think that they matured into well-educated, successful women, replete with careers, husbands, children, and pets. But I've never forgotten that afternoon, and have, over the years, devised my own well-thought-out wishes to put to that genie.

For my first wish, I asked the genie to arrange it so I would need less sleep. It seemed to me that whenever I stopped moving, I fell asleep. Of course, I never took into account that I got up at 5 a.m. and spent the next 17 hours doing what everyone demanded of me.

The genie finally heard my wish for less sleep, so he gave me insomnia. Now I regularly awake at 3 or 4 a.m., ready to conquer the world. Fortunately, our home is configured so I can entertain myself without disturbing everyone else. By the way, if you think daytime TV is bad, you should try it this early in the morning. It's so bad it usually puts me to sleep in my chair—which was the purpose of turning it on in the first place. Despite bad TV, I suppose I should thank the genie for granting my first wish.

I can remember being cold as far back as I am capable of remembering. All of the "normal" people vowed the thermostat was where it was supposed to be, and often implied that there was something wrong with me. Since no one was willing to jack up the heat a degree or two, I amassed a wonderful collection of sweaters. People would make a point to drop by to see what pretty sweater I was wearing that day. One especially cold and cranky day, I asked the genie to make me as warm as all of those normal people.

The hot flashes started the winter we lived on Maryland's Eastern Shore, the winter when we had a record 18 inches of snow. I didn't tell anyone about my hot flashes; for those few private moments I would be blissfully, blessedly warm. I'm sure my secret smile puzzled my husband, but like most men married for a certain amount of time, he had learned not to ask.

We moved back to Amelia Island that May, and I soon armed myself with pills to control my out-of-whack thermometer. Despite this artificial aid, I have warmed up to within the normal range, and people no longer have to stop by to see what pretty sweater I am wearing. Thank you, Genie—I think—for granting my second wish.

As I remember it, school seemed to have involved a great deal of singing. The occasional odd looks I garnered while warbling away didn't really register until my mother signed me up for violin lessons after she discovered my grandfather's forgotten fiddle. That's how we learned that my ear is a quarter note flat. (I'm sure that poor teacher went to her reward years ago, and I do hope the Good Lord had a special place in heaven reserved for her.)

By high school, my friends had made it clear that none of them wanted to be near me as I butchered whatever we were singing. When a girlfriend and I conned our parents into paying for ballet lessons, I discovered that I have this wonderful sense of rhythm, as well as a certain facility on the dance floor. That discovery helped my bruised ego, and I gladly began to mouth the words to various hymns and anthems I was faced with.

I repeatedly petitioned the genie to retune my ear, but he ignored me for years. Then I fell in love with Persian music during our short assignment in Tehran, but it took me months to figure out why. I'm sure that those of you who are musically inclined can explain it better, but Persian music is in a minor key that makes it sound a quarter note flat to most people. That, of course, makes it sound just right to me. For once in my life, I could hum along without everyone writhing in agony.

I guess two out of three wishes granted isn't so bad; I should be thankful my intermittent insomnia allows me some extra time to myself, and my age-adjusted thermostat means that my life is no longer a battle to stay warm. As long as I merely mouth the lyrics, no one need ever know that I sound like a rusty air raid siren.

8 October 2004

Turning One Corner after Another

"**E**at your crusts, Cara; they're the best part."

I looked down at my plate and started laughing. Upon it rested the remains of my lunch: two right angles of toasted bread. (OK, so maybe they were a couple of degrees off, but what's a degree or two to an English major?) I had called those two bits of bread "corners" ever since I was a little kid.

It took me decades to realize that while I had been busy growing into a potatoholic, my mother would always be addicted to bread. I think it was actually painful for her to allow those two corners to lie dormant, unloved and unwanted. In my insensitivity that day, I reminded her that she'd tried for 60 years to get me to eat the two corners of every sandwich she'd ever served up. "Besides, Mom, that's what dogs are for," I said to conclude my rebuttal. With no effort at all, I conjured up a vision of the lunch-time vigil that Patootie posted regularly until I had forked over first one, and then the remaining corner of my sandwich.

There was always something on these corners to titivate a puppy's palate—a schmear of tangy mustard, a sliver of cheese or baloney. Sweet grape jelly along with peanut butter was always welcome. A special treat for both of us was what I call the Weight Watcher's hot dog. Long ago, I learned to appreciate the subtle flavor (as in none) of the turkey hot dog. Weight Watchers taught me to nuke it, slice it lengthwise, and place its prone form on the bottom half of the slice of diet bread I'd cut in two. Liberal amounts of mustard, relish, and onion contribute no calories or points. But they do contribute to the smacky sounds that a puppy makes when all of that tanginess hits her taste buds. Yum, Mom!

If I didn't eat fast enough, or she thought I was in danger of forgetting her (fat chance, you should pardon the expression), she would edge closer, lick her lips and produce a long, martyred sigh. Some days, if Horatio and his CSI team had a particularly intriguing case to solve in Miami, my eating pace would grow slower and slower. Patootie's drooling chin would almost be in my lap before I came to my senses and slipped her a corner.

Patootie was supposed to have been a small and delicate ladylike dog with a wispy coat and an eagerness to please. What we got was 45 pounds of attitude who knew the precise moment to turn on the cute. That was usually a nanosecond before we strangled her for committing some unspeakably messy crime. Her short coat brought me further down the road of self knowledge. Thanks to this little dog, I realized that I am lucky to get my own hair combed each day; having to comb someone else's as well would pose a daunting logistical challenge.

And, oh yeah; she fell paw over tail in love with Andrew the minute she saw him. For a while, I called my husband "Elvis," because Patootie sat in open-mouthed adoration right in front of him, just like all those teenage girls swooned over Elvis back in the 1950s. I swore that she would trample her way over my broken and bleeding body to sit at his feet. Except, of course, when I had corners to offer up.

But Patootie is with us no longer. Thank you, Doctor Hicks and your wonderful staff, for making that sad day go as smoothly as possible. With her demise, I have yet to find a good use for my corners. I have threatened to stick them in the freezer until I find a suitable replacement for Patootie.

So hang on, Talullah; I know you're out there somewhere. I'll start looking for your ten pounds of puppy love any day now. This time around, I want someone I can carry around, someone who will curl up in my lap on a nice rainy day. Gone are my visions of a fluffy little dog; I'll take a short coat, thank you. And this time, you'll fall in love with me, instead of our Adult Supervision. He can get his own dog. I can't wait to start teaching you to eat corners while we watch schlock TV. When we find out whodunit, I'll switch over to the classical music channel so we can take our post-prandial naps.

In the meantime, I chuckle every time I think of St. Peter sitting down to lunch at the Pearly Gates. About three bites into that oh-so-heavenly sandwich, he's going to look down to find two beady brown eyes watching him closely. And even he will eat a little faster when Patootie sighs and moves in a little closer, impatient for that tasty corner.

1 June 2007

One Blanket Too Far North

I want it clearly understood that I am not normally a cranky person. There are, however, certain notable exceptions, this time of year being one of them. Now, don't get me wrong; I think that our autumn days have their own special beauty. I love fall colors, and it's nice not to be damp around the edges most of the time. We can open the windows and let the ocean breezes displace the air-conditioned atmosphere. The very rhythm of our days changes, too, as we fall back to standard time; some chores left until a summer's evening are now shifted to morning's light. We are fortunate that fall doesn't arrive until November.

No matter how late it may be, fall inevitably leads to winter. And winter means short, dark days with temperatures 30 to 40 degrees too cold. No wonder I'm cranky; winter is for people who don't have either the money or the sense to move to a warmer climate.

The sleet was horizontal the day we left Norfolk to move down here. While I was happy to be moving farther south, I was disappointed that I wasn't going to Tampa, as I'd requested. It wasn't the first time that the Navy had ignored what I'd wanted and had given me what I needed instead. When I was a newly hatched officer, I asked the Navy to send me to Naval Air Station New Orleans. I'd live in the French Quarter and buy one of those low-slung Mercedes-Benz sport coupes as my first car.

I ended up at Naval Air Station Pensacola, living in Bachelors Officers Quarters and driving a baby blue Volkswagen named Clyde. I also met a naval aviator named Andy or Randy—I couldn't remember which—who was just back from Vietnam. When I eventually confided to him that I was supposed to be living in the French and not the Bachelor Quarters, he explained that Navy New Orleans is 50 to 60 miles from the Quarter, and that the monthly payments on the Benz I wanted would probably be double my paycheck.

Years later, the Navy once again gave me what I needed instead of what I wanted. Despite my best efforts at both cajoling and bullying, the Navy couldn't find me a job in Tampa. I'd been there several times and I had grown to like it more each time I'd visited; besides, it was much warmer in the winter than Norfolk. I came dragging home the day I was told I'd be receiving orders to Kings Bay, Georgia, and shared the bad news with my husband. I missed the twinkle in his eye when he assured me that we would live on Amelia Island, and would somehow muddle through. It only took me a couple of months of island life to realize I'd landed in Paradise, except—paradise or not—it's at least one blanket too far north for me.

So come the Autumnal Equinox, I get a little cranky. I envision the next few months when the wind blows out of the frozen north instead of the balmy south. Months when I battle my husband—and the Labrador—to boost the thermostat higher than the artic setting they prefer. Even with my age-adjusted body thermostat, I cover myself with layer after layer of clothing and search the cupboards for last year's box of low-cal hot chocolate. My skin crackles and withers from all of the hot showers, while my Adult Supervision mutters about the water and electric bills.

To compound the problem—and ratchet up the crankiness—we always travel north to see family and friends over the holidays. Once we reach our destination, we discover that we have entered a black and white world: black, bare tree branches and dirty white snow. (The Iranians call snow *barf*—with good reason!) My lip sticks out in a permanent pout as I remember that Amelia Island is still in Technicolor: green palms and pines, red poinsettias, blue sky and ocean.

After about a week of frigid black and white, I start screaming, "Get me back to my island!" Unfortunately, my snit continues even after our return, because December is followed by the two Slit-Your-Wrist months. We're in for days and days of gray skies and a cold rain that are guaranteed to dissolve even the most cheery mood.

Cranky person or not, I'll tell you one thing: If I'd been Persephone, I wouldn't have spent the winter in Hades looking for my daughter. She's a bright kid; she can find her way to our hotel in Tahiti.

19 November 2004

Watch Out for Fulminates, Snits and Fervors

We have something in our house called Fulminate of Andrew. All of us, including the dogs, try to avoid activating it. During the spring of this current political season, we find that it is usually fired up during the evening news—or by CNN any time of the day. Andrew's fulminate does not transport him anywhere, but holds him quite comfortably while it squats in the living room and emanates sulfurous clouds of adult language.

I am so adept at recognizing this fulminate for what it is because of something Ed McBain explained in his 1986 murder mystery, *Cinderella*.

"Years ago, when there were still some laughs left in their marriage, he and Susan defined a 'huff' as a small two-wheeled carriage. A person who went off in a huff was therefore a somewhat lower-class individual who could not afford to hire or own a 'high dudgeon.' A high dudgeon was one of those big old expensive four wheelers. A person who went off in high dudgeon was usually quite well off. A person who was in a 'tizzy,' however, was truly rich since a tizzy was a luxurious coach drawn by a great team of horses to a stately mansion called 'Sixes and Sevens.' All at Sixes and Sevens were in a tizzy save for Tempest, the youngest daughter, who was in a 'teapot.' A teapot was even smaller than a huff, about the size of a cart, but fitted with a striped parasol…"

Thanks to Mr. McBain's tutelage, I can not only recognize Andrew's fulminate (a dark beaker of a rumbling, fizzing mixture) but can also realize that I am traveling about in a "snit," which is a small scooter that emits an irritating buzz. A "funk," on the other hand, is a self-propelled motor scooter. A "blue funk" is the upscale version; it is painted the appropriate color, with tassels on the handlebars. And a "fit" is merely a turbo-charged snit.

The last time I found myself in a "pique," I realized this small boat-like craft could only be propelled in silence, with my lips pursed and my beady eyes slitted against the bright light of reason. When I descended from my pique, I wrapped myself in a "sulk," which was a large gray blanket that afforded no comforting warmth.

Our small, auxiliary dog jumps stiff-legged into her "hysterics" every time a strange dog appears. An hysterics is similar to a pogo stick, in that it only travels vertically, accompanied by sharp, percussive sounds. The Labrador retriever, on the other hand, occupies his "oblivion" most of the day. An oblivion is available to both man and beast, and is a low, overly-padded couch. It can be moved, but only with much difficulty and a great deal of moaning on the part of the occupant.

I have learned over the years to avoid people who are in a "fervor." Those unfortunates usually experience a rapid heartbeat, exaggerated gestures, and a runaway mouth. It takes the fervorite an inordinately long time to recognize his predicament, let alone escape from it.

A "paroxysm" is even worse. It is a pit into which the unwary fall during moments of great emotional upheaval. Those who fall in lose control of their extremities and tear ducts. And, far too often for the comfort of those around them, their voice boxes short out to emit only shrieks of unremitting pleasure or pain.

The most terrifying conveyance any of us can mount is a "rage." It is a large black vehicle not unlike a military tank; it spews great belches of fire from its turret as it annihilates everything in its path, even cockroaches. The person who eventually emerges from a rage often has little recollection of the preceding events, and is amazed at the sometimes irreparable damage that has been inflicted during the ride.

The next time you start to fall into a "fury" or go on a "tear," remember the qualities of the vehicle you are about to board. It could very well be the worst ride of your life. As for me, I shall sit quietly and draw the curtains closed around me in my "solitude," and read a little more Ed McBain.

19 April 2004

Has Your Fun-O-Meter Pegged Out?

The way I figure it, we're all ready for a sensory deprivation chamber right about now. If you're reading this, you have survived, more or less, the excesses and depredations (yours as well as other people's) of the just-completed holiday season. That's the good news. The bad news is that we are about to embark on what used to be my most unfavorite time of year.

I have hated January and February for as long as I can remember. By the time these two dreary months roll around, I am always fat and broke, thanks to the aforesaid holidays. I hate it when the number that registers on my bathroom scale is larger than the number that's displayed on my check register. The weather is yukky, and the only bright spot we can look forward to is St. Valentine's Day, a minor celebration at best—and another fat attack at the worst.

But lo and behold, good St. Nicolas brought me an unexpected present this year. I found it quite by accident as I was sweeping up the Christmas debris— ripped wrapping paper, empty gift boxes, and plundered money holders. It was a small object wrapped in plain brown paper, with a curious shape. It weighed almost nothing. It had my name on it, so I stopped what I was doing to sit down and unwrap it. (No hardship there; I hate housework almost as much as I dislike being fat and broke.)

My chubby little fingers finally exposed what was to be my last and best Christmas present, the one that more than makes up for the electric fork and the Slim Whitman CD Santa Claus handed me this year. It's a brand-new Attitude! It sat purring in my hand for a moment while it got its bearings. Then it looked around, all bright-eyed and bushy-tailed, and promptly canceled my annual Depression Celebration. Next, it canceled my Slit Your Throat Session, and even deleted the week listed on my calendar as Bored Out of Your Gourd Days. Blah had been banished!

January may be National Oatmeal Month, but there's no law against putting sprinkles on it. Just because it's also National Diet Month doesn't mean we have to eat twigs and berries; surely someone has invented a low-cal/low-carb hollandaise sauce by now.

This year, my new Attitude and I invite you to join us in regrouping, regenerating, retooling so when we emerge from winter's dark tunnel, we'll be svelte and rested, ready to celebrate spring and summer.

First, we start by enjoying the plain and healthful fare we must now fix ourselves. A fist-sized piece of broiled nothing sounds wonderful after Aunt Tootie's triple-decker gut bomb. And skipping the starches altogether is an excellent idea, especially since one self-satisfied hostess quietly announced at her holiday feast that she had substituted half-and-half for milk in the mashed potatoes and cream gravy.

Next, we gently reintroduce our bodies to the

concept of moving vigorously enough to work off some of our extra avoirdupois. After being confined to one sort of conveyance or another in our travels to family and friends, it almost feels good to stretch and move. Even those of us who are philosophically opposed to exercise find it pleasant to take a stroll after spending several days sitting on various couches, recliners, and stools. You may have noticed that the tables next to all of these aforementioned seats were filled with bowls and platters of calories. Some were of the crunchy, salty variety, while others were the sweet gooey kind. I have found that the liquid kind, especially if it's from the grain group, is particularly nefarious. I hate to admit it, but it feels good to get back to the exercise program I complained about so bitterly before the Christmas Fatathon.

After clogging our appointment books or PDAs with meetings to organize holiday bazaars, parties, musicals—not to mention our attendance at same—now's our chance to enjoy all that empty space on our calendars. Now we can read a book, go for a long walk, or heaven forfend, sit quietly and vegetate. "Vegetate" reminds me: I now have the time to admire a pot of vegetable soup as it festers all afternoon on the back burner.

I figure it will take at least a couple of months before the needle on my Fun-O-Meter moves out of the red danger zone, so I'll refrain from offering you calories on a cracker if you do the same for me. You'll see my body in the spring, when it's lean and rested.

Ciao! (You should pardon the expression.)

2 January 2004

The Right Rules Make Life Easier

Life is hard, they tell me. They also tell me that it gets a little easier if you follow the rules. The trick, I have discovered, is to find the right set of rules. Some people are fortunate enough to find their rules early, and are set for life. Others of us embrace and reject different rules until we discover a workable combination. At this late stage, I define "workable" as something that keeps me out of jail and still gives me a shot at Heaven. That I can look myself in the mirror every morning is a welcome perk.

I ran across Nellie's Rules several years ago, and thought they deserved more than just a passing glance. Like I do the rest of the rules I've encountered, I pull them out periodically to see if they're still pertinent. Some have stood the test of time, while others have degenerated into nothing more than a good chuckle. Here they are; see if you agree with me.

Never take a sleeping pill and a laxative on the same night. Whoa, Nellie! (To coin a phrase.) This woman is in serious need of more adult supervision than I am willing to give her.

There can be a fine line between "hobby" and "mental illness." Spelunking and skydiving come to mind.

People who want to share their religious views with you almost never want you to share yours with them. Amen, sister.

You should never confuse your career with your life. Your "In" box will never investigate something that goes bump in the night, and your PDA could care less that it's your birthday.

No matter what happens in life, somebody will find a way to take it too seriously. Stay away from these people.

Nobody cares if you can't dance well—just get up and dance. Yeah, but sing off-key on karaoke night, and they will jerk you off the stage. Does that mean dancers are kinder than singers?

Never lick a steak knife. Refer to my comments about Nellie's first rule. I still have serious reservations about this woman.

Take out the fortune before you eat the cookie. That's probably because the fortune is often the best part.

The most destructive force in the universe is gossip. The second most destructive thing is not being privy to it.

Nobody can give me a clear and compelling reason why we observe daylight-saving time. This one's easy; so it's still light enough to mow the lawn when you get home from work.

A person who is nice to you but rude to the waiter is not a nice person. I agree, but given some of the service I have received over the years …

Your friends love you, no matter what. Be sure to reciprocate.

As good—or as amusing—as Nellie's rules are, they don't quite cover all of the pitfalls inherent in our daily life. Here are my additions to her list that help me live happily ever after in Paradise:

Bloom where you're planted. We don't care how you did it in Cleveland.

Make lemonade. This is a No Kvetch Zone.

Don't try to make lemonade for someone else. They'll complain about that, too.

Make sure your glass is always half full. A half empty glass is guaranteed to make you cranky.

Get up an hour earlier. You will be organized and in control for the rest of the day.

Go to bed an hour earlier. I bet you've forgotten what it's like to wake up rested.

Kill your television. Read a book! Go for a walk! Talk to someone!

Never continue a relationship if your pet disapproves. My cat bit one person in her 18 years, and that boyfriend turned out to be a real nogoodnik.

Procrastination has its own rewards. Slow down and serendipity will happen.

29 August 2003

Discovering New Rules for Old Age

A friend and I were sitting at one of our favorite watering holes the other day—having a glass of milk, of course—when I bemoaned the fact that the aging process is not only down a slippery slope, but a bumpy one, as well. "You know you're getting old," I observed, "when you rely on your pill caddy to tell you what day of the week it is."

We laughed at that, and ordered another milk. "Even my dog has a pill caddy," I admitted. "He and my husband take their glucosamine chondroiten together every morning!" That keeps the days straight for Andy, but I'm not too sure our 11-year-old Labrador cares one way or the other.

My most recent insight about modern maturity comes thanks to Rees Snedaker asking us to write about rules and laws for the August meeting of our writers' group. You know the kind of thing he had in mind: Don't swim for a half an hour after you eat; your face will freeze with that scowl on it; wear clean underwear in case you're in an accident.

Long past the age when adults quoted rules about eating and swimming (or anyone cared about the state of my underwear), I realized that life had taught me the following new rule: *That part of your body that now hurts will stop doing so when another part of your body becomes unhappy.*

My right hip had been aching for months, so when my annual checkup came around, I asked the doctor to investigate it. The X-ray revealed the barest start of arthritis, nothing that Tylenol couldn't handle. So I stopped worrying and complaining and popped a pill whenever I planned to put a lot of stress on my hip. (You know you're old when you have to take a pain reliever after doing the Twist and the Frugg with Midtown's '60s band.) And so things hobbled on, until I moved my shop from Ash to Centre Street this May. By early June, my left foot was killing me; I had overextended the ligaments on the top. That was when I realized I had spent hundreds of hours going up and down ladders or standing on them to shelve thousands of books. And when I wasn't standing on a ladder to shelve books, I was perched on one to paint everything red, white, and blue. As I popped yet another Tylenol to relieve the foot pain, I realized that my hip hadn't hurt in weeks.

I limped along with my sore foot until bronchitis hit. Another visit to the doctor. He should give me a frequent flyer discount! About a week into antibiotics and antihistamines, I noticed that my foot no longer ached. That meant I wasn't hobbling when I went from bed to couch and back again. The bronchitis eventually disappeared, but I had an irritating cough left over as a reminder.

The cough went away during the afternoon I spent with ice packs and pain pills after oral surgery. (A surgical procedure, I might add, that seems to be a rite of passage for mouths that have been around as long as mine.)

I can now chew on both sides. I have no cough. My lungs are clear. I no longer limp from a sore foot or wince from a disintegrating hip. I can't wait to find out what will sabotage my body next. You were right, Dad; old age ain't for sissies!

27 September 2002

Repeal the Law of Inertia!

I have never taken part in a political demonstration, but I just may have to mount a one-woman campaign to convince our lawmakers to repeal a law that poses a real threat to our productive way of life.

For decades I attributed my unfinished To Do lists to laziness and procrastination. I lived with this dirty little secret for years, hoping that no one would notice that I did not accomplish all that I set out to do on any given day. I was too embarrassed to ask if any of my friends suffered from the same deficiency, and it never once occurred to me to search for a support group so I could talk to my own kind.

I finally broke down and confessed my problem to my Dearly Beloved, who suggested that I was not underachieving, but overscheduling. What a wonderful relief to know that there was such a simple solution to my problem. He reminded me that I am retired, and that I am no longer required to fill every waking moment doing something productive. That's why, he explained, that I turned in my type A suits to Buy-Gones all those years ago. Now I'm supposed to be a type R, for Relaxed.

This is not the time for me to take a quick sniff to smell the roses; now I should find a comfortable bench in the garden, and spend several long moments contemplating their beauty.

I made my To Do list as usual the next morning. Then I ripped it in half. I spent the rest of a very delightful day slowly and peacefully accomplishing the few things I set out to do. I could now afford to pay attention to those pesky little details that always make the difference between a good job and a great one.

All went well for several weeks, until my malady reappeared; I had only accomplished a fraction of my newly-shortened list of things to do that day. It was only then that I realized that I am not a slacker, but a victim of one of the more insidious laws of nature: The Law of Inertia states that bodies at rest tend to stay at rest. I cried with relief and joy at this discovery. I was not a bad person! It is this awful law that forces my backside to remain glued to my oh-so-comfortable wing chair. It is this law, not any defect of my own, that forces me to remain seated, watching schlock TV for hours instead of bestirring myself to be a productive member of our island society. I could cry all over again when I think of the shirts I could have ironed, the volunteer work I could have done, and the walks I could have taken, if only I had not been struck immobile by this unfair law.

When I first became aware of this law and its effect on me, I thought to call Larry Myers to ask him to approach Aaron Bean in Tallahassee about getting this dreadful law repealed. But the Law of Inertia crosses state lines, which makes it a federal matter. I'm in trouble; I am nobody, and I don't know nobody, especially in Washington. I'll have to do it the hard way—make the dreaded cold call on one of my congresspeople to remind him that I voted for him so he could represent my interests up there where all of the big kids play.

Right about now, I imagine that those of you with a more scientific bent are opening your mouths to remind me of the second part of the Law of Inertia: Bodies in motion tend to stay in motion. Well, Smarty Pants, if you'd read the fine print, you would have discovered the Universal Exception to this part: Bodies in motion tend to stay in motion until after they've celebrated a certain number of birthdays. After that date—but before the expiration date of the body in question—a combination of arthritis, bad knees, and a slight increase in avoirdupois, cancel this part. This, in turn, renders the first part into an unmoving (you should pardon the expression), immutable law. That puts me right back where I started, sitting instead of doing.

Our only hope is my plan to petition our emissaries in Washington to have this law repealed. I'll pack my bags and be on my way—just as soon as I get up out of this chair.

9 March 2007

Anniversary a Time for Review

$\mathbf{M}$y husband attributes the longevity of our marriage to having separate bathrooms. The occasion of our 30th (Yikes!) wedding anniversary seemed to call for an in-depth review of tactics, such as separate bathrooms, that have proved to be successful over the decades.

I like to tell people we met in a bar. My mother's scandalized addendum that it was a VIP reception at the Officers' Club in Pensacola, Florida, merely adds an extra fillip to the story.

We were both confirmed bachelors, and wed only after years of dating. I'm not too sure who was more surprised at the ceremony: the bride and groom or their attendant families.

Our honeymoon did exactly what it was supposed to do; it got us (really well) acquainted with one another. And taught us that this marriage could be saved only by each of us having a bathroom of our own. We had been solitary bachelors much too long; no sooner would one honeymooner repair to the "necessary," than the other would be writhing in abject need. Needless to say, the newly minted Curtins endured several less than romantic moments during their first week of living happily ever after.

One of my friends confided to me several years ago that she thought that I alone had decreed the separate bath rule. She complimented me on this ploy to maintain a certain amount of mystique in my marriage. My enamored spouse would never discover the unguents and potions I applied during my toilette in order to present a perfumed and powdered façade to all the world. Although the number of unguents has increased and the duration of the toilette has lengthened, I resent her implication that without this ritual, my visage would frighten small puppies.

While the separate bathroom theory has its points, I contend that having separate checking accounts is the secret to our marital success. I have thus avoided the pitfall of trying to convince my husband to pay for expensive crystal when he is of the opinion that discount retailers offer a perfectly good alternative. A $10 wineglass, after all, holds its liquid as well as a $50 glass.

I'm sure, that after 30 years, he's figured out that I'm not buying Waterford at Wal-Mart, but he graciously declines to make an issue out of it.

Nor does he demur when I bring home $500 worth of sale merchandise and loudly announce that I've saved myself $150. He just reaches for one of those Waterford glasses and fills it with amber liquid in response to what he affectionately calls my "female finances."

Speaking of finances, I knew I'd been right to maintain a separate checkbook when he began to refer to it as "The Black Lagoon," a quagmire created by my own arcane accounting methods. His last foray into it was an attempt to discover why the bank said I had several hundred dollars more in my account than I did. He emerged several days later and reached for yet another Waterford glass. I was directed to the bank and its professed expertise in this area. The bank haughtily announced its figures were correct and there was no need for it to wade into the Black Lagoon. So be it.

Regardless of my funky fiscal practices, nice accessories have regularly appeared over the years as if by magic; my dearly beloved has ostensibly given little thought about the amount of money that has exchanged hands for that particular *objet d'art* to appear in our home, and I have had the pleasure of acquiring it.

We broke that two-checkbook rule when we lived overseas, and I still grumble about it. Every two weeks, the Navy would dump my Lieutenant's pay into a joint account. And for the first time in our marriage, my Adult Supervision became aware of just how many unbudgeted purchases I was wont to make during any particular pay period. Given my own Waterford glass of amber liquid, I am confident I can come up with a list of the unique detritus we do not own because of too much supervision. I assure you that one of the first things I did upon my return to America was to establish a separate, unsupervised pot of money.

Our review session almost at an end, I recalled a recent conversation with my parents upon their 62nd anniversary. Mother quietly announced that she no longer knew whether she still loved my father, or if he had become a bad habit she couldn't kick. Daddy just chuckled, safe in the knowledge that either way, he was home safe. Andrew and I have agreed that, bad habit or not, we're stuck with one another. Besides, whoever files for divorce is automatically awarded custody of our canine Demonic Duo.

12 September 2003

Do You Play the Name Game, Too?

$\mathbf{B}$ack in November, when I was talking to Kerry Woods about her newly-relocated Buy-Gones consignment store, I asked her about the wonderfully whimsical flamingo who graces the enterprise. You see her on the side of the new building, on business cards, and scattered throughout the shop. While my customers and friends bring me red, white, and blue mementos, Kerry's present her with flamingos. But as popular as she is, this lady flamingo doesn't seem to have a name.

I discovered a similar deficiency when I gravitated from Kerry's flamingo to Tom and Jenny Bishop's carousel horses at the Bailey House. As I took pictures to accompany my December column, I discovered that each horse had a distinct personality. I also discovered that none of them has a name.

Who would name a flamingo, or a carousel horse, for that matter?

Uh, that would be me. It's a talent (?) I inherited from my dad. He named the family car after a character in a popular song of the day, so when I acquired my first trusty steed, I spent a great deal of time selecting the perfect name for him—Clyde. And so it went from Clyde II (Clyde the Tooth) to my current ride, Othello.

I eventually gained a reputation for naming things; a friend's Volkswagen was named Gladys, and I dubbed Andy's Cutlass Supreme Mildred the moment I met her. Years later, Andy had trouble selling her; she was a "luxury" car with a too-large engine and a straight stick. The Volvo salesman scarfed her up in a heartbeat. He planned to sell her to a wholesaler who'd pass her along to a moonshiner in the Carolinas. I couldn't wait to hear that some "Revenoor" had filled her fat, snooty fanny with buckshot!

I've even named a commode. I dubbed him Leon in honor of the best "gotcha" artist I ever met. Leon (the commode, not the man) piddled water on the floor, but we never figured out when or why Leon would fail to hold his water. The oddest thing was that Leon would only piddle at night, so sometimes we would get our feet washed while attempting to conduct other, more important, nocturnal business.

It was when we moved to Florida that I realized my penchant for naming inanimate objects was not limited to cars or commodes. The first thing I named when we moved into our Fernandina home was the water heater. But before I tell you about that, I have to explain a little about our house.

By the time we became the proud owners of our current abode, the garage had been converted into living space. The garage door had been replaced by a brick wall and casement windows. Behind three louver doors were hidden the usual impedimenta found in garages: water softener, furnace (one of two, as I found out later) and the infamous water heater. Because it was tucked behind a door, it took us several months to discover that it was sinking through the floor. We placed a panicked call to a local plumbing outfit. The diagnosis was a disaster: our rapidly disappearing water heater was so fat that the plumbers doubted they could get it out of the house. One frustrated plumber wondered how anyone had installed the thing in the first place.

The answer was simple; this industrial-size water heater had been wheeled in on a dolly through the original garage door. At the end of a day filled with sweating, swearing men and gouged walls, we dubbed it Godzilla, the Water Heater from Hell.

We'd moved in during April, so several months passed before we turned on the heat. That's when I discovered Vulcan, the (second) furnace who lurked in our attic. One cool autumn evening I innocently pushed the proper buttons; the furnace clicked on, emitted a *WHOOSH*, and then clicked off. The repairman explained the whooshing sound came from the open flame that Vulcan was spewing across the attic insulation. We replaced him with a heat pump who squats in the back yard. I named him Falstaff; he's short and round like his namesake. Both man and machine are famous for their prodigious appetites; Shakespeare's character loved his ale, and our machine gobbles kilowatts with unholy gusto.

I suppose it's only fair to warn you—assuming you haven't already figured it out—that I am as apt to ask the name of your air conditioner as I am to wonder what you've named your kids or pets.

30 January 2004

(Im)pertinent Words to Make You Stop and Think

Most of my mornings in Paradise start with watching the pelicans troll for their breakfast along the surf line while I have that all-important first cup of coffee. My mind slowly spools up to remember the day's planned schedule of work, errands, food, exercise, and fun. I know that all of those things will happen, but not necessarily in that order.

And so it went, one bright and shiny morning not too long ago. I had awakened with the dawn and had started the quiet rituals demanded by dogs, coffee pot, and the laundry monster that lurks in our utility room. I retrieved the newspaper from the end of the driveway—no use asking the Labrador to do it; his face was smushed in his food bowl. At 13, his interests lie in two important body processes, one involving intake and the other output. The rest of his day is spent napping until it's time to do one or the other.

A small sigh of satisfaction escaped as I finally settled in my favorite chair to enjoy my coffee and the ubiquitous pelicans. Something in the newspaper caught my eye; I scanned the short article, then lowered the paper and smiled.

The DVD in my brain took me back decades to my parents' old black and white television set. On it flickered the beloved Victor Borge as he delivered his stunning monologue about how nonsensical the English language is. Lord knows, it ain't sensical.

"If America has forefathers," he had wondered all those years ago, "why weren't there fivefathers?"

I knew it was going to be an especially irreverent day, perhaps even an irrelevant one. For that matter, Victor, why couldn't we have had foremothers? Threemothers? Even at that early hour, I was in touch with my feminazi side. While I'm at it, why do we always talk about our forebears? Why not fivebears? And what's with the bears? What's wrong with opossums or raccoons?

Now my brain was awake and humming. Newspapers, puppy dogs and pelicans were long forgotten as I began to expand on Victor's premise: If I know one person with impeccable taste, I mused, I am bound to know several whose taste is merely peccable. And one friend, who shall remain blessedly nameless, has atrocious taste. Come to think of it, what is a trocious, anyway? Short and squat wearing clashing stripes and checks, I should think.

Yet another of my acquaintances considers himself to be an iconoclast. I guess that makes me a dyed in the wool (not cotton or nylon) conoclast. Does his different philosophy make him an outcast? Perhaps he's really an incast and it's the rest of us who are out.

This language and philosophy conundrum calls for a spot of quiet reflection. But if one person in the group intrudes upon your solitude, do the rest of us merely trude? While most of us are real people, sometimes there are impostors among us. Does that mean that the rest of us are nothing more than plain old boring postors?

My mind soared with new linguistic possibilities. I suppose it's better to be impressed than pressed. If to importune is to be rude, perhaps portune is merely vasive, rather than invasive. With apologies to Jack Heard and the famous Oxley-Heard Funeral Directors, wouldn't you rather be balmed than embalmed?

I try to be tolerant of my neighbors, but under- and over-achievers merely whelm me at this stage in my life, and if your mind is less than invigorated by all of the foregoing verbiage (as opposed to nouniage), perhaps we could safely say you are merely vigorated.

If you are reading this right before you imbibe at happy hour, perhaps you could be a wee tad more temperate today and merely bibe. After all, we are long past the stage of trying to outbibe one another, aren't we?

If you think that you've been floored by all of this wordplay (or is it wordwork?), who's to say you haven't been walled or ceilinged? Instead of feeling cornered by this question, you could just as easily feel curved, or even—heaven help us—squiggly.

Regardless of how this column has made you feel today, it's rather amusing to realize that this bit of writing is both pertinent and impertinent at the same time.

23 April 2004

Just Wear a Smile and a .38

*B*ump. Did you hear that? What was it?

The Navy trains its spouses to cope with long periods of solitude while its men—and now women—go to sea for months. Those of us left behind are expected to manage the house, the cars, the kids, the pets, and our jobs without letting our absent partner know any of the sometimes unpleasant details that might distract him or her from the important business of defending our country. The same rules apply to things that go bump in the night.

Crick. I was amazed to learn that many of the other wives returned to their parents or moved in with one another for the duration of the six month cruise. *Scrape.* I was a naval officer, and didn't have any of these options; I was expected to report for duty every day, neat, clean, and with a smile on my face.

I soon learned that I was well suited to long bouts of solitude. I immersed myself in work, and spent my small amount of leisure time in projects and hobbies. Unlike the majority of the other wives, I was not afraid to stay alone. *Raaassp.* As the years went by, I began to cherish my time alone; our reunions were fun, and we had so much catching up to do. *Thunk.*

By the time we retired to Paradise, we had each grown used to a certain amount of separation. *Sssss.* Thanks to our absent partner, we could now turn the TV and the climate control to the settings we wanted; we could choose a dinner menu that would gag our Dearly Beloved. We could hog the bed and eat the last of something lurking in the refrigerator without the fear of reprisal.

The downside of all of this solitude, of course, was that we were in charge. *Skitter.* There was no one to turn to when we were suddenly awake in the middle of the night; did our sleeping brain hear something that shouldn't be there? *Plink.*

Andy's job with TraumaOne required a certain amount of traveling. No problem; I had long ago learned how to cope. Besides, I took great comfort in the two guard dogs we now included as part of the family. The black Labrador retriever was large and imposing—unless you knew that as a breed, they are playful oafs who never met anyone they didn't love. Our last Lab was the soundest sleeper I've ever met; we knew that some day a burglar would trip over him and sue us for bodily injury. *Chink.*

Our mutt, on the other hand, was small and frightened; I assured myself that she was a barker and could at least alert me to imminent danger. It was up to me to decide whether she was barking at a grasshopper or the Mongol hordes beating the front door down.

Somewhere along the way, we took Gary Belson's Basic Pistol Course with Defensive Tactics. As my fellow graduates know, his course is much more than teaching you how to point and shoot a firearm. *Tap, tap, tap.* Gary talks a lot about home security and how to make it a little harder to become a victim of the predator class. He will, upon request, come to your home to show you specific measures you can take to feel safer, be safer at home.

Andy was in Kansas City when something went *Bump.* I muted the TV and listened. Nothing. I turned up the sound, but soon heard another odd sound. I'd made the security check hours ago, and knew that everything was closed, locked and bolted. Our beloved Labrador was long gone; the 15-year-old guard mutt slept peacefully at my feet, but at this stage in her life, she's apt to sleep through the Apocalypse.

The third time I heard something strange, I muted the TV and retrieved one of my deadly little friends from a nearby hidey hole. I'm sure I was an impressive sight in my ratty bathrobe and scuffed slippers as I assumed the modified Webber stance and went from room to room. I also modified an old advertising slogan: *Just wear a smile and a .38.*

I stood back and to the side of ground floor windows in darkened rooms to peer outside. Nothing. The dog slept on while I checked deadbolts and window locks. Nothing.

I returned to my chair and the TV, but I kept my friend close by, just in case. I took her with us when I escorted my sleepy dog on her bedtime trip to the back yard. I locked and bolted the door behind us, gave the dog her last treat of the day, and returned my Smith & Wesson to her hiding place. I climbed the stairs and put her sister, Big Bertha, on the bed beside me in Andy's spot. I drifted off into a peaceful sleep, uninterrupted by any strange sounds.

The moral of this story is twofold, Gentle Reader: If you haven't done so already, sign up for Gary Belson's course; the dates and times are always announced in the *News-Leader*. And second? Don't play any pranks on me at home, especially after dark, sweetheart.

5 January 2007

PEOPLE, PLACES
& THINGS

History Unfolds on Stroll in Bosque Bello

I suppose it's because my relatives are so scattered about the eastern half of the United States that I missed learning about one of life's more comforting duties. The first time Cindy Glenn took me with her when she went to visit her family's graves, I thought it was an odd way to spend an hour or two of our vacation.

But several years and visits later, I have come to appreciate these quiet moments, so much so that I now visit Bosque Bello from time to time. When I paid my most recent visit on a bright Monday afternoon, I turned off of North 14th Street onto the entrance lane named Bosque Bello. It dissects the new section of the cemetery, which opened in 1945. I followed the lane straight back to the small cinder block structure at the intersection; behind that building lies the original cemetery, which had its entrance off of 8th Street. Vestiges of the original iron gates delineate the division between these two sections. Unpaved lanes, such as Magnolia, Oleander, and Redbud, criss-cross the property, with the boundary road appropriately named Perimeter.

Located in a grove of ancient oak and cedar just north of McClure's Hill, the wood is festooned with

Spanish moss and resurrection fern. Dappled sunlight illuminates some graves, while others rest in the shade. It is not meticulously manicured, but celebrates the glory of our Southern flora. No one is in a hurry here, so I took my time reading inscriptions and paying my respects to people I never knew.

Local historians disagree about the origin of Bosque Bello. Some, like Hal Belcher, cite documents that attest to its existence in 1798. Others, whose accounts can be found in the files at the Amelia Island Museum of History, recount the story that Don Domingo Fernandez, holder of the Spanish land grant for this area, donated the land to the city for use as a burial ground.

Whatever its origins, Bosque Bello is a repository of our history, both ancient and current. The oldest grave documented so far is that of Peter Bouissou de Nicar, laid to rest in 1813. One of our newest belongs to Lieutenant Edward John Kent Johnston, Confederate States Navy.

Lieutenant Johnston is not the only Civil War veteran to be found here. There are almost 50 others, including Major Thomas Leddy, who was head of the military police when Union forces occupied the town. Like many of his fellow officers, the Major remained in Fernandina at the end of the war, and at one point owned the Florida House Inn.

I eventually found Amos Latham (1761–1842) on Oleander Lane. This veteran of the Revolutionary War became our first lighthouse keeper when the light was moved here from Cumberland Island.

Lest you think that our cemetery is the repository for only those far removed from our daily lives, even the quickest of visits will introduce you to names on our lips every day. Lasserres (early auto dealership, real estate) have been buried here since 1877, the Waas family (pharmacy) since 1881, and Ferreiras (insurance, real estate) since 1883. After the turn of the century came the Higginbothams (city and county governments) in 1900, the Mizells (as in Mizell Avenue) in 1916, the Tringali family (shrimping) in 1920, and the Litricos (shrimping, *Amelia Now*) in 1925.

Should you wish to add your family to this impressive gathering, Ed Deely is the man to talk to. He can be reached through the city's Public Works Department. Since we've been using Bosque Bello for around 200 years, I was a little concerned about available space. But Ed assured me that a new section has just opened, so there will be no problems in the foreseeable future.

If you'd like to know more about our cemetery, visit the Amelia Island Museum of History, talk to Hal Belcher, or buy his definitive book on Bosque Bello. It's available through the Amelia Island Genealogical Society.

8 November 2002

"That Was Easy!" in Colonial Virginia

The last time Cindy Glenn and I visited my dad, we went through three pounds of coffee and a six-pack of toilet paper. (There has to be a significant psychological message here, don't you think?) When I called Dad to tell him we were on our way to see him again, he laughed and promised to stock up so we could use both pots in comfort and style.

I soon dubbed our trip to Virginia and parts north the "That Was Easy!" tour. I installed one of Staples' famous Easy Buttons on the dashboard, and gave Dad a button so he, too, could render editorial comments about the challenges and distractions that life sometimes poses. He grasped the concept quickly, and the button is now background music when we chat on the telephone. "That was easy!"

Our next stop on this East Coast Fatathon was Williamsburg, with side trips to Jamestown and Yorktown. It had been years since my last visits, and I was impressed with how much these historical/tourist spots had metamorphosed over the years.

There was much more to see and do than I remember from my coed days at William and Mary.

(Don't get excited; I majored in recess at W&M. I dropped out, grew up, and got my English degree from Old Dominion College [now University] in Norfolk.)

During my long absence, Williamsburg made the Duke of Gloucester Street a pedestrian mall, with the Wren Building at one end and the Colonial Capital at the other. Between these venerable piles of brick are now an almost endless array of things to see, to do, to buy, and to eat—of course!

We hit the Easy Button often, after finding a parking place, walking from one end of town to the other, and trudging up steep staircases designed to meet 18th century building codes.

It was gratifying to discover that the college had preserved many of the campus landmarks I remembered from my youth. Of course, the Wren Building classroom where I learned to write Shakespearean sonnets is now an off-limits administrative space. The Sunken Garden was the way I remembered it, and still divides the campus. These days, everyone thinks it quaint that the girls' dorms are on one side of the campus and the boys' were built on the other.

While the town has changed, some things have remained constant through the centuries. The Kings Arms Tavern is still illuminated solely by candlelight, and its peanut soup and Sally Lunn bread are as good as ever.

Our tour of the Governor's Palace reminded me that people used to use their entrance halls to display their impressive arsenal of weaponry. This array of swords and muskets told us right away that we'd better treat our host and hostess with respect, or suffer the consequences. In my student days, I'd taken many tours of the palace, and was now proud to point out quietly some of the more subtle decorative touches that the docent failed to mention. I had also spent many "study dates" in its formal gardens on Sunday afternoons; the docent and I laughed about the peacocks that used to guard the grounds—sometimes too well! I guess they finally chased one too many visitor. I remember watching one afternoon as one of the big males chased a portly gentleman who'd gotten too close with his camera. I had no idea that peacock—or that pudgy tourist—could run that fast!

As much as I enjoyed Williamsburg and the college, I was most impressed with what they've done with Jamestown. While Williamsburg celebrates life in the 1700s, Jamestown represents the colonies a century earlier—and what a difference a mere 100 years makes! We were met by our docent, who dressed and talked and acted like John Rolfe, the man who married Pocahontas. For over an hour, he led us from place to place at the Jamestown Settlement, and he never stopped talking. He filled our heads with a wealth of information about some of the first English men and women who arrived on this continent, as well as the chieftains and their tribes who watched them as they waded ashore.

At the end of each fact-filled day, one of us would smack the Easy Button, and search out liquid therapy followed by an early dinner.

If you are planning to attend Jamestown's 400th Anniversary in 2007, I have a few pointers for you: Take comfortable clothes and shoes, bring money, and leave the hot, tired, and very vocal small children at home.

Next time, I'll tell you about visiting our nation's capital with no adult supervision—"that was easy!"

19 May 2006

A Country Mouse Goes to Washington

I feel like such a country mouse every time I go to D.C.: all of those sharp-looking men and women in their finely-tailored power suits, talking earnestly into their cell phones; the neat shops in Georgetown with goods that are either too small or too expensive for me; the bartenders and waiters who are too cool to pay much attention to a chubby matron from flyover country.

Washington was to be the culmination of our "That Was Easy" tour, and Cindy had worked hard to make my first unsupervised foray into the big city a success. I made only two requests: I wanted to see and do and eat everything, and wanted to avoid the aviation museums. (Almost every holiday season, the Curtins travel to the capital only to go back and forth between visiting relatives and the Smithsonian's Air & Space Museum.)

First on our agenda was lunch with a friend at Union Station, a place that always reminds me of the airport scene in *Men in Black* where Tommy Lee Jones and Will Smith watch intergalactic visitors come and go. The day of our visit to Union Station, I swear I saw a left-eyed Venusian sitting at the bar.

I discovered Chinatown by reading a Metro map, so we added it to our agenda. They really do have those dead, scrawny ducks hanging in the windows! (I had always wondered if those shops were real, or if they were merely a product of some scriptwriter's imagination.) We went in what I can only call an apothecary, and came out giggling, our noses filled with scents we'd never sniffed before.

The next day started early with an appointment with a baby panda, and I'll share with you a secret we discovered quite by accident: The zoo grounds open at 6 a.m., so get there as early as you can—the animals are awake and frisky! But bring your own coffee, because the concession stands don't open until 10. We got there at 8, and watched the panda and its mother at their morning ablutions, and then strolled over to watch five cheetah yearlings having an early morning game of rough and tumble.

Next we took a teary stroll through the World War II Memorial, followed by therapy at the Willard Hotel's glorious round mahogany bar. This was one of the few days Cindy drove us into the big city, and I marveled at her ability to find a legal parking place close to the hotel. That parking space proved a lifesaver later as we scurried to the car; Cindy maneuvered us into a hasty retreat, and we watched the country's first large immigration march in our rear view mirror. The only thing between us and them was a D.C. cop car with all of its lights and sirens going. That was easy!

We were sufficiently recovered the next day to visit the Botanical Gardens—early in the morning, of course. That left us plenty of time for lunch and my first tour of our nation's Capitol. I'm glad I took lots of pictures, because there was just too much to absorb in an hour and a half.

As much as I was enjoying our stay, I had been biding my time for our visit to the Library of Congress, and I almost cried when we had to leave. I loved everything about it—the smells, the art, the architecture, and the mere thought of all of that knowledge in one place. And it all started with Thomas Jefferson's donation of most of his library. The collection was kept in the Capitol, and after the British burned it during the War of 1812, Mr. Jefferson again supplied the starter stock for our nation's library. It gives me goosebumps to think about it. We spent most of the morning at the library, and then met friends for a leisurely lunch. Next on the agenda was a much-needed nap.

That nap was the smartest thing we did all week, because we had a date at 7 p.m. A friend of a friend was going to give us a private tour of the White House, and it would turn out to be the highlight of our trip—even better than the Library of Congress!

Drat! I'm out of space! Next time, I'll tell you all about the Country Mouse at the White House!

2 June 2006

A Country Mouse
Visits the White House

It was the sixth day of our stay in the D.C. area, and both Cindy and I were beginning to feel the effects of this whirlwind visit. Early each morning, we'd get up and out, riding, driving, and walking from one breathtaking spot to another. I can honestly say that I was not disappointed at any of the places we toured. They were all beautiful, clean, and well maintained by their knowledgeable and enthusiastic staffs and volunteers. Once again, I was proud to be an American, and thought that my nation's capital was a magnificent showcase for our heritage.

Now it was time for a well-deserved nap after lunch. We wanted to be at our best when we presented ourselves at the White House at 7 pm. We set several alarm clocks; neither one of us wanted to be late for this important date. Refreshed and dressed in our best, Cindy drove us there; once again, she miraculously found a legal parking spot, this one close to the designated guard shack.

It was a lovely evening, and we stood outside while we waited for Senior Chief Clark to collect us. He was a friend of a friend, and had graciously agreed to lead us on this private tour after his normal 10-hour work day. I don't know whether he's head of the Navy Mess that feeds the staff at the White House, including the President and Vice President, or if he's just one of the staff. But the way he quietly handled issues that arose during our visit—and the alacrity with which his subordinates followed his orders—told me that he was high in the pecking order.

I could feel the change in the air as we stood admiring the sunset from the guard shack's steps. Then I heard the sirens. I looked behind us at the Capitol Police officer we'd just been talking to, and he nodded: "You're fine, ladies; just stay right there."

The sirens grew louder, and five (I counted them) motorcycle cops preceded a very black SUV, two large black limousines, and another SUV. The tail end was a D.C. Police car. Gates swished open and the cortege sped by. I thought I saw a hand wave behind tinted glass, and fought the automatic reflex of coming to attention and popping my sharpest salute. It was Vice President Cheney, on his way to the farewell dinner President and Mrs. Bush were hosting for Supreme Court Justice Sandra Day O'Connor. The Country Mouse was speechless.

The Senior Chief collected us just as my heart had settled to its normal rhythm. He showed us his spotless galley, and I marveled at how much it resembled one aboard ship: a small, immaculate stainless steel space with everything in its labeled cubbyhole.

His cell phone rang as he was letting us poke our heads into the Executive Dining Room. "You ladies have a seat in here for a moment while I talk to this guy," and he was gone. Cindy and I proceeded to give ourselves a tour of the room. Its beautifully paneled walls were filled with paintings of famous ships and battles, and I felt as if

I were in a large, well-appointed wardroom aboard ship.

We sat—gingerly—at one of the tables. My camera recorded each of us sitting there among the Presidential china. I helped myself to several sugar packets graced with the Presidential seal.

Soon the Senior Chief was back and continued his talk about menus and who sits where; I had chosen the chair that the President usually sits in. I was stunned for a moment, but recovered enough to squirm and twitch so the maximum amount of my backside came in contact with the same blue leather that holds the Presidential posterior.

His telephone rang a second time, and the Senior Chief disappeared again. I looked at my watch; we'd planned an hour tour, followed by dinner at some trendy spot. With travel time, we figured we be at the restaurant at a fashionable 8:30 or 9 pm. That time table was rapidly disintegrating.

The Senior Chief did not return for some time, but he sent one of his staff in with dessert and coffee, served on Presidential china, of course. Our cameras came out again to record the heart-stopping event. He returned just as we were sopping up the last raspberry glaze with chocolate brownie crumbs. Stop me the next time you see me, and I'll explain the story behind this signature dessert that's served at the White House.

The dessert was fortuitous, because we didn't leave the premises until around 9:30. We were both exhilarated and exhausted. Our cameras were filled with photos, including those of us behind the Press Secretary's podium with the White House logo as backdrop.

There came another stir as we were on our way out. "Hang on a minute, ladies, while I see what's going on."

He was back in a moment. "Hang loose, ladies; be cool."
That's how the Country Mouse got to shake hands with
Chief of Staff and Mrs. Andrew Card.

The Country Mouse fell dead into bed that night,
but she made happy, squeaky sounds as she slept.

23 June 2006

If It Walks Like a Duck ...

I walk like a duck.

It all began the Monday after the Shrimp Festival, when I awoke with an irritating hitch in my gitalong. I was leaving for Australia in three days, so I took two aspirin and told my 21-year-old body to shape up.

I hobbled my way through airports in three countries and waddled all over Australia. Along the way, I discovered that an extra dose of aspirin and an extra glass of wine did wonders for my mistreated hip.

I could barely walk three weeks later when Tim Merrill met us at JIA with one of his stretch limos from North Florida Limo. Bless you, Tim. Too bad the stretch pulled into our driveway at midnight; it was much too late to impress our sleeping neighbors.

I called Dr. Warren Groff the first thing the next morning. (In case you've lost track of him, he's moved to Baptist Primary Care in Kingsland. Now he has a smaller, more personalized practice, which I think you will enjoy. Call him at 912-882-3737 for directions.) His initial diagnosis was a pulled muscle in what we will euphemistically refer to as my hip. (Just because one owns a derriere doesn't mean one should talk about it in public.) The Darvocet he prescribed didn't erase the pain entirely; I was mellow, but I still walked like a duck.

Someone suggested deep massage, and I hesitated to allow someone to knead me like bread dough. The only masseurs I've seen were in old black-and-white "B" movies, and I just knew the person doing the kneading would be 400 pounds of Nordic muscle.

Fortunately, Judy Bunner did not live down to my movie stereotype. Instead of a supersized Nordic blonde, she turned out to be a trim brunette who patiently listened to my tale of woe before she started kneading. Her ministrations, coupled with the soft music and soothing décor at Amelia Massage Associates, produced the most comfort I'd had in several weeks.

I met Jeff Hall on my second visit to Amelia Massage Associates, and his kind attentions further reduced the pain in my posterior. I must admit that I became a little worried when he gave me a hot herb pack on the appropriate spot. I was afraid to ask what the greenery was; if he'd replied rosemary and thyme, I'd have to start looking for the apple to stuff in my mouth before he pulled a Brownin' Bag over my poor, battered body!

My next adventure in Paradise came at the very talented hands of Jana Diaz. She's the clinical supervisor at the Rehabilitation Services of Baptist Medical Center Nassau, just north of Amelia Massage Associates on South 14th. (It is a small island, after all!)

After listening to the saga of my sitter-downer, Jana began the laying on of hands. She's a graduate of the University of St. Augustine and holds a master's in Physical Therapy. From the way her eyes lit up when she talked about her profession, I knew I was in good hands, you should pardon the expression.

Jana quickly determined that one side of me was pointing north, while the other side pointed south. Yet another part of me was just plain ol' whoppy-jawed. We can't pin this condition on any one mishap, so I have chalked it up to lots of years of fast living.

Jana and her talented hands have worked miracles. I can now duck-walk my way—sometimes with the assistance of a cane—through most of my daily routine. While I will take most of the summer to fully recover, I am once again living happily ever after in Paradise.

Now that I am able to get out and about, I would be remiss if I neglected to say thank you to Publix and Wal-Mart for their electric buggies. Without them, I would have been unable to deposit significant portions of my retirement check into their coffers. I have told the staffs at both places that they should encourage every customer to use these buggies; you are so comfortable in them that you expand your visit, as well as your expenditures.

Besides, the buggies are fun to drive, although my skills behind the controls put a new meaning to the label "woman driver." While not politically correct, it is an unfortunately accurate description of my careering from one aisle to another. I thought about trying for wheelies in the parking lot, but I want to come back and play with their toys again.

For the moment, I walk like a duck with a cane, but those days are numbered. And I can assure you that the next person who quacks when I go by is gonna get thwacked by said cane. Perhaps I should have said that I now walk like a duck with a cane—and an attitude.

30 July 2004

"Aunt Bea" Does Virginia Beach

The telephone call that all adult children dread finally came, and I raced to Virginia Beach to be with my father as we said goodbye to our emphysemic wife and mother. My dear friend Cindy also raced north to be with us, and I don't know what we would have done without her. I have thanked her profusely in private for her help and support, and now I thank her in public.

I tried to stay on my Weight Watchers diet, but food is love. Who could turn down my Dad's hot homemade bread slathered with butter and marmalade? Or thick braunswager sandwiches washed down with beer? Each night we ate in, Dad offered us a cooking lesson and a repast that filled all of our empty corners and crevices. And the restaurants he took us to were his favorites because of their reasonable prices and generous portions. I was doomed.

After a particularly long and difficult afternoon, the three of us were very tired and discouraged. We went straight from the hospital to dinner at Dad's favorite cafeteria, and I found myself chowing down on comfort food like a field hand before the sun had set. The dinner revived us, so I asked Dad if he knew of a

nice neighborhood lounge where Cindy and I could go
for a nightcap (at 8 p.m.!). He drove us by Tony's, not
two miles from home.

We switched cars and drove back to check out Tony's.
There weren't many customers, but the bartender—a
young woman in jeans with a kerchief on her head—
smiled nicely, so we climbed on two empty bar stools.
I quietly explained that my mother was very ill, and we
needed some liquid therapy after a difficult day.

Some time later, we asked for our check, which the
bartender presented while asking if we felt better. "Yes,
this therapy session has helped a lot; thank you."

"I should hope so," she said. "I've been pouring
you doubles!" I left her a generous tip, and hoped that I
could make it out of there without embarrassing myself.

Too late. Tony's had filled with regulars while I had
my back turned on the room and the pool tables. When
I swung around to put on my heavy coat, I interrupted
a very serious-looking young man at the nearest pool
table as he drew back his cue to aim a powerful shot.
Even I know that interfering with someone's pool shot
is instant death. I must have made a little squeaky sound
as I clutched my coat to me, because he straightened
up and turned around to face me. Leather vest. Tattoos.
Scraggly beard. *I'm dead*, I thought.

"I'm terribly sorry. Excuse me," I quivered.

"No, ma'am; excuse me!" and he stepped aside so
Cindy and I could have a clear path to the door.

As we scurried out, I noticed yet another evil-
looking young man. Since he was as big as a refrigerator,
I quickly deduced that he was the bouncer. By this time,
I had donned my too-dressy gray Chesterfield topcoat
with its velvet collar and huge glittery pin; he checked

out me and my bling in a heartbeat. He gave Cindy the once-over, and then he got the most angelic look on his face: "God bless you, ladies."

At last, my gray hair was worth something; we were gonna make it out of this place intact, as long as I kept my ditzy blue hair act together. So I put on my best imitation of Opie's Aunt Bea and smiled and nodded at everyone I encountered.

We made it to the front door, only to find it blocked by more louts standing around outside. They were muttering at each other and practicing their mean looks. One of them spotted us, and he melted into a sweet kid who opened doors for his elders. "Right this way, ladies!"

"Oh, thank you, dear. My, it's gotten quite chilly, hasn't it?"

"You ladies have a nice night!" came from the middle of the pack.

Cindy and I made it to the car and locked all of the doors before we howled like banshees at what we'd gotten ourselves into. "Did you see the expressions on their faces?" I asked Cindy. "They looked at us like we were their Sunday School teachers!"

"No!" Cindy gasped, "Their grandmothers!"

24 March 2006

A Guy's Guide
to the Last Party of the Year

Coming up with a bright idea for this column, not to mention the crafting of all of its witty repartee, is similar to inventing a tasty dinner night after night. Both require a large inventory of ideas and ingredients, as well as a sure hand in blending the disparate elements into a smooth and entertaining feast for body or spirit.

Fortunately, I am experienced enough at wordsmything to know how and when to employ one of the traditional, sure-fire aids for harried writers: plagiarism. When you read voraciously as I do, you are bound to run across something now and then that's worth stealing.

I won't tell you the name of the book that inspired today's masterpiece, because it's been out of print for at least a decade. With my luck, the author's mother lives on the island, and will recognize every word I have lifted from her gifted child. Suffice it to say that in the middle of this small volume of witticisms, I unearthed a guide purporting to help the males of our species survive their New Year's Eve dates. The guide explains that long after the guys thought that the dreaded Senior

Prom Disease had been eradicated, it morphed into the equally debilitating New Year's Eve Malady.

All over the planet, women are muttering about this last night of the year. "Do we have reservations? Should I take bail money with me? Do I need a smallpox booster?"

At the height of their delirium, some women hallucinate an ideal New Year's Eve date that requires at least one change of clothing, Dom Perignon, and watching the sun rise on a beach that's several hundred miles more tropical than the one we currently occupy.

Those of us who have survived our youthful fantasies about this night now merely demand to be allowed to dress up and take the good jewelry out of the safety deposit box. We also expect to be kissed at midnight, and to be driven home by the person we came with. And, last but not least, we expect someone else to get up at 6 a.m. to let the dogs out so we can groan and roll over.

But, according to this author I am plagiarizing, women do not usually have a good time on this last and first bash of the year. Luckily for everyone involved, amnesia sets in quickly, and the writer assures us that we will be eager to repeat the whole sordid process next year.

Women all over the world will have forgotten, he says, that most of us had a good cry in the car, either going to or returning from the evening's festivities. We will be tricked once again into drinking New York champagne instead of a tastier and more expensive vintage. And once again, we will barricade ourselves in strange bathrooms until we either do or don't get rid of the four pounds of canapés we consumed along with the domestic champagne.

Those of us who are truly unlucky will spend the remainder of the evening trying to come up with a plausible explanation of why we are missing at least one item of that expensive jewelry we demanded to wear.

He also forgot to mention that at least one other woman will be wearing the same thing that we have on, and even worse, she paid less for hers than we did. We will need a suicide watch if it turns out to be not only cheaper, but a size smaller. He also failed to reveal that this is the night you discover that the really cute guy in your circle smells funny up close and is a slobbery kisser.

Nor did that author remind you that after two helpings of lobster Newberg and several glasses of the much-maligned champagne, your dearly beloved's boss turns into Shrek's ugly brother. His wife, on the other hand, remains stone sober, even after copious amounts of bubbly, and whinnies like a horse at your escort's lame jokes.

He also forgot to warn his compatriots not to congregate in small clumps across the room to talk about work and sports. This activity, he should have explained, irritates us women to no end; we prefer that our men spend the evening chatting (whatever that means) and dancing with us, especially to the more exotic rhythms.

Despite the best efforts of everyone to teach them better, the men will magically reappear from their various dark corners to claim their dates as the band announces the last dance. A quick twirl around the dance floor and you're out the door. If we didn't cry in the car on the way over, now's our cue to cry on the way back; we've finally realized that if we women had any sense, we'd send the men to the party so they could talk about guy things, and we'd stay home and eat takeout in our jammies. Please pass the Moo Shoo Pork.

31 December 2004

Don't Touch That Dial!

I am alive to tell you my latest adventure thanks to the good Sisters of Saint Benedict. They used their rulers on my husband's knuckles until they taught him not to kill chubby gray-haired matrons who have irritated the living bejabbers out of him. Thank you, Sister Ethelreda.

I have admitted many times that I am one of those unfortunate electronically challenged people. Any device with more than an on/off switch is yet another mystery of the universe, as far as I am concerned. I thought of my long, frustrating history with gadgets the other night as I admired all of those colored buttons on the remote control for our television set. Andy was busy with the Civil Air Patrol at the airport, parking the airplanes of our Superbowl visitors. Now was my chance to explore all of those buttons, and at last correct my electronic deficiency.

To condense the next 45 minutes into a few sentences, I had, in that time, entered every one of our most-watched channels into the Favorites category. Since I was too tired and sleepy to be witty, I entered a really easy, boring PIN.

The next morning—the Friday before the Superbowl, I must note—I turned on our television, hit 36 for Headline News and provided the PIN when asked for it. "Invalid PIN" was now plastered across the screen. I had the same result when I punched up Fox News. And the History Channel. And every other channel I had entered into the Favorites program. Only now did I notice that the icon displayed looked like a padlock, rather than a heart. Heaven help me; I had locked the Curtins out of every single channel they liked to watch.

Thanks to Sister Ethelreda, my Adult Supervision did not strangle me on the spot when I confessed what I had done. (By the way, confession may be good for the soul, but it don't do dip for your marital relations.)

I had already revised my morning to substitute a visit to the Comcast office on 14th Street for the errands I had originally planned to run. I waited patiently until Lorena was available at Comcast. She had dealt with me before and seemed to find my attempts to master digital television amusing. She started smiling when she saw me; I imagine she thought she was in for a chuckle. She got more than she bargained for when I told her, "You have to help me save my marriage."

I had the undivided attention of everyone in the Comcast office, both staff and customers, as I regaled them with my electronic adventures, my amateur attempt to control trons, the night before.

In between guffaws, Lorena determined our television had a bad control box; I should have been able to unlock all of those channels as easily as I had locked them. She quickly wrote a work order for a technician to restore these channels. The other thing that saved my bacon (plus other parts of my anatomy) was that I had not locked us out of the channel that was to carry the game.

Lorena looked at me a little strangely when I asked to borrow the office telephone at the end of our negotiations. "You don't think he'd give me a cell phone, do you? I'd probably dial Bangladesh by mistake and not know how to turn the silly thing off!" She dialed the number for me, and then passed the receiver through the small opening in her service window. When Andrew growled hello, I quickly explained that the tech would be at our house the next morning. I swear his response of "Very well" sounded more like "You live."

A very nice young man showed up the next morning, made our remote go boop-beep several times, and left. Our viewing pleasure was once again unlimited. Shortly after that young man's departure, I received my remedial remote control instruction. It is now indelibly engraved on my brain: the Curtins only need to turn on the television, VCR and DVD players. We need to adjust the volume. Upon occasion, we need to hit the pause button on the VCR or DVD. And we need to know how to turn everything off. The rest of those pretty buttons are just there for decoration.

And Lorena? The last time I saw her, she had her head cradled in her arms on her desk, laughing uncontrollably. I have that effect on some people.

25 February 2005

Come Meet Rudolph, the Red-Nosed Cessna

I have always encouraged my husband in his dream to own an airplane. I knew that we could afford a boat that we could eat and sleep on, but we'd never own a plane with similar capabilities.

After we had driven up and down I-95 for the 45th time, Andy quietly announced that he was going to find a better way for us to travel from Paradise and back again. We started by renting aircraft that our friends owned, and I was amazed; instead of an 11-hour drive to Virginia Beach, we arrived after a three-hour flight.

After several years, we ran out of friends with planes. When the last plane was sold, the Curtins were grounded until the Laylands, the Otts, and the Curtins went in together to buy Rudolph, our very own Cessna 182. That's called a partial ownership, and given the Curtins' political proclivities, I am wont to say that the part we own is the right wing.

Flying a small plane is very similar to piloting your own watercraft on the Intracoastal Waterway. First, we both begin and end the day's trip when we're ready, instead of having to shoehorn ourselves into some commercial carrier's schedule. When we stop along the way for food and fuel, we are greeted by people who want to work there, are interested in our craft and its instrumentation, and want to know where we've been and where we're going.

And, of course, everyone talks about the weather. No convenience store clerk along the interstate ever treated us that way.

But most important of all is that the ICW, like our nation's airways, is far less crowded with other vessels that can get in our way or threaten our safety. And I know that many boaters, like all pilots, undergo rigorous training programs that far exceed any DMV requirements for the drivers we encounter along our nation's highways.

Andy and I, along with Rudolph and his red propeller hub, have taken a couple of short trips this summer. Planning for the first trip started out to be the $100 cheeseburger. You know how that goes: "Let's take the boat to St. Augustine for lunch." By the time you pay for gas, lunch, and depreciation, that C note is history. We initially planned to fly down to Ocala for our $100 cheeseburger. (The restaurant at the FBO has all sorts of aviation memorabilia that I love to look at— and the food's good, too!) Somewhere in the planning process, we decided to add a night at Cedar Key, then home the next day. It was a nice treat after a rough spring.

Early in August, Andy flew us to Cordele, Georgia, and then drove us to Lake Blackshear Resort. The food was delicious, the grounds were beautiful and uncrowded, and the accommodations were spacious—we even had a lanai! The resort is on the Georgia Veterans Memorial State Park, and we visited its museum and outdoor displays the day we arrived. The next morning we went to Andersonville National Cemetery; I was moved by its mute testimony, and surprised to discover that it is still available to 21st century veterans.

When we first started renting planes, I gave Andy the Ken Burns' Civil War videotape set. We spent that winter watching and learning. When a friend in Detroit decided to get married several months later, we wanted to visit some of the places we had studied. Andy flew us to Shiloh, Chickamauga, and Gettysburg on the way up and down.

Another similarity between marinas and FBOs is the animals. One place we stopped on our way to the wedding had a kitty asleep on top of the warm computer monitor. When we were ready to leave a small FBO in Ohio, the manager had to find Sam, his basset, because she loved to fly. The week before we arrived, she'd crawled into the back seat of a local pilot's plane and fallen asleep. She woke up halfway to his business appointment, and he'd had to do a U-turn to bring her back!

We left Cordele, and spent the next night in Beaufort, South Carolina. It was our first visit to that fine old Southern lady, but not our last. Savannah was our next full stop, with a visit to Kevin Barry's Irish pub and dinner at the Boar's Head. After beignets and eggs at Huey's the next morning, we pointed Rudolph toward Paradise.

While I am not a pilot, I can assure you that I have learned to earn my keep on these jaunts, even if my new nickname is "Ballast."

26 August 2005

Trip of a Lifetime—
Separate Vacations Together

I am convinced that my husband and I just took separate vacations together.

We agree that we both took the same interminable trip together from Fernandina Beach, Florida to Brisbane, Australia—via DFW, LAX, and Auckland, New Zealand. That portion of our Vacation of a Lifetime could occupy this space several times over. Travel is no longer the romantic adventure it used to be; now it is a royal pain in the posterior. And don't get me started on all of the alphabet soup agencies you have to convince that you don't have a communicable disease or a rabid political agenda before you are allowed to enter and/or travel in your own country.

Once we arrived in Brisbane, however, our goals and recollections began to diverge. Thanks to the fine example set by Dave and Carolyn Ashcraft, we had signed ourselves up with Goana Air Safaris, located at the aerodrome (I love that word!) at Redcliffe, just outside Brisbane. If you are a pilot and can fly a Cessna 172, you get yourself to Brisbane, pass your check ride, and Goana hands you one of its Cessna 172s. You and your companion then proceed to fly, along with the other people and planes in your tour group, to a series of pre-selected destinations throughout the eastern portion of Australia.

So when my pilot husband talks about visiting Down Under, he talks about flying to 15 locations and the 16 take-offs and landings he made. (He's carefully explained to me that the number of landings must match the number of take-offs. It has something to do with the fact that take-offs are optional, while landings are mandatory. Who makes up these rules, anyway?)

And he'll go on to tell you that in 14 flying days, he accrued 31 hours of flight time and covered approximately 3,300 nautical miles. We used paved, gravel, dirt, and grass runways. At the Avington sheep station in the heart of Queensland, we parked our planes in the front yard, where normal people would park their cars.

Speaking of Queensland, the first photograph I took in that wonderful country was of an automobile license plate: "Queensland—the Sunshine State." I had traveled many hours and many miles just to go from one Sunshine State to another!

Given half the chance, Andy will regale you with trekking to the springs in Alice Springs, waltzing with Matilda in Winton, finding the Southern Cross at the Cosmos Centre in Charleville, and finally snorkeling in the Great Barrier Reef off of Brampton Island.

I, on the other hand, have a slightly different memory of our three weeks away from Amelia Island. I am willing to try almost any unfamiliar food, except insects, of course. And I leave my vanilla ice cream and cheeseburger palate behind when I travel. (The mango ice cream on Brampton Island was quite a treat!) Breakfast buffets included all of the standard fare, plus spaghetti and something that looked suspiciously like Campbell's baked beans. I watched carefully one morning as a young woman in her power suit built a breakfast of toast with a fried egg on top, and then covered them with a generous dollop of those baked beans. I'll pass, thank you.

And Australian coffee is to die for; it's very, very strong and very, very tasty. I was an addict by my second cup, and I miss it to this day. My next gustatory adventure was in Alice Springs. I ordered the Bushman's Lunch and received a platter of emu paté and grilled kangaroo steak. It was delicious, but I have discovered that most of my friends don't know what an emu is. Think ostrich, only smaller and uglier. One tried bullying me out of my lunch one day, but he never stood a chance.

That particular emu and I met during the highlight of my version of our vacation of a lifetime—our visit to the Lone Pine Koala Sanctuary in Brisbane. I got to hold (and I am not making this up) a real, live koala bear! His name is Conrad and I have our picture to prove that we were cuddle buddies, even if it was for just a few minutes.

When people ask me what my favorite city on the tour was, they are surprised when I tell them it was Coober Pedy, down in South Australia. Even though this small town is in the heart of the opal mining district, opals are not the reason this place stands out; Coober Pedy is simply the most unusual town I've ever been in, including several locations in the Middle East.

First, it looked like a moonscape, with not a tree or blade of grass to be seen. Next, it was pocked with man-sized holes drilled in the never-ending search for opals. Barren holes are left empty and unfilled, deadly traps for the unwary.

But it was our motel that truly fascinated me. The Desert Inn was drilled into the side of the mountain; our subterranean room had no windows or pictures on its stone walls. Since all of that rock is such good insulation, the rooms were equipped with neither heat nor air conditioning. And it was quiet. Very quiet. Stone is a wonderful soundproofing material.

And when we turned the lights out after yet another very full day, my Adult Supervision did not put up much resistance when I asked for a night light.

G'night, mate.

9 July 2004

Visiting the Outer Banks— and Getting in Touch with Your Inner Princess

Boy, have I got a story for you! Pour yourself something good to drink and get comfortable. I slipped my leash last month, with predictable results.

Cindy Glenn invited me to share a week in her timeshare on North Carolina's Outer Banks. It had been a long time since my last visit there, so I jumped at the chance. Besides, my husband could use a break from his onerous duties as Adult Supervision.

When we finished our planning, Cindy's one-week sojourn had grown into 14 fun-filled days of going up and down the East Coast. We left Fernandina one bright morning with everything two women could possibly need over the next two weeks.

We checked into her timeshare and used several tourist brochures to plot our week; we had places to go and shops to visit. And of course, there was breakfast, lunch, and dinner. Coffee breaks. Happy hour.

We hit Kelly's Restaurant and Tavern one night, and therein lies my tale. Why are you not surprised that it involves food and liquid therapy? We'd cased this Nags Head restaurant during our travels up and down Route 12, going from Corolla and its lighthouse in the north to Jockey's Ridge and Manteo to the south. (I'll have to show you my tee shirt from Duck, North Carolina; it's a hoot!)

Kelly's was a lot larger than it had looked from the highway, and the dining rooms (note the plural) were decorated with all sorts of dead fish and game. We both ordered seafood; Cindy had Crab Remik (a satiny tomato and cheese sauce), and my broiled flounder was world-class.

We entertained ourselves by checking out the other diners, as well as the décor. The long table in the middle of the room was filled with grungy young men. We were surprised, because Kelly's seemed much too nice to attract the scruffy crowd. We finally decided that they were serious young men whose work required them to live rough. Perhaps they were marine biologists living aboard a research vessel, or archeologists camping at a dig. Lord knows, that area attracts both professions.

We were well into our main course when a very nice gentleman came by to ask if our meal was satisfactory. Indeed it was, and we quickly determined that he was Mike Kelly, the owner. We complimented him on his establishment and his menu. We were savoring the last few bites of our dinners, when Mr. Kelly appeared again. Yes, we assured him, we were going to have a nightcap in the tavern. He escorted us there.

A young man was sitting at a table near the tavern's entrance. I noticed him only because he glowered at us so ferociously as we sailed by. I dismissed him from my mind; we were with the owner, so no one could mess with us.

The tavern was filled with people, and everyone turned to see what royalty Mike Kelly was escorting. They watched as he selected our table and summoned a waitress. Chrissie explained that Mr. Kelly was buying the first round; she urged us to have something special. We both chose Bailey's Irish cream. What else would we order in an Irish tavern?

The young man playing acoustic guitar on stage did not offer his own songs, but covered those written by famous artists. If I'd closed my eyes, I would have sworn that the original artist was there, and not this young man in a stocking cap and tee shirt.

In between sounding like Billy Joel, Elvis, or Bruce Springsteen, he told us how grateful he was to front for the band that would appear at 10 p.m. The crowd was eclectic—the young, as well as blue-haired grandmas; sport coats and ties, but blue jeans, too. Security was large men with sunglasses and their heads on a swivel.

Suddenly, Cindy pointed at the stage. The marine biologists and archeologists from the dining room were the 10 o'clock band! So much for our profiling talents. Speaking of talent, if we'd thought the young man in the stocking cap was good, these guys made him sound like a croaker! Mr. Kelly appeared again, asking how we liked the band; when we told him that they were wonderful, he beamed and said, "They're from Richmond!" Perhaps Richmond, Virginia, is the NYC for Bankers.

Even the heartiest of party girls gets tired, so we signaled for our check. Mr. Kelly appeared again to hold our coats and escort us to the door. Those who were not diving for our prime table stared at us, still wondering what royal house we represented.

The angry young man was still at his table as Mr. Kelly ushered us out. As we thanked him for our enjoyable evening, I overheard that young man collecting a $13 cover charge! Mr. Kelly's gracious escort service had robbed him, and he was not pleased.

The two princesses from Amelia floated home and dreamed of gracious Irishmen, marine biologists, and cranky young men who wanted to take our money.

'Nite, all!

6 April 2007

Wardrobe Malfunctions Can Happen— Even in Paradise

I was chest deep in preparations for our Vacation of a Lifetime this May when I realized I had a problem. It would take approximately 30 hours for us to fly from Jacksonville, via Dallas and Auckland, to Brisbane, Australia.

I had already solved the usual traveler's problems of dehydration, blood clots, personal hygiene, and reading material during this extraordinarily long trip. Stark terror hit the day I realized I would spend all of that time with the same brassiere wrapped around my body. And it would be even more than 30 hours if you started counting from when I dressed in Fernandina to when I finally undressed in Brisbane.

I can assure you that I rip that bit of lace and elastic off of my body at the earliest opportunity, just like every other bra-wearing woman you know. The prospect of wearing it for 30-plus hours gave me screaming fits.

I confided my trepidation to a friend, who recommended I wear a sports bra for the duration of my plane ride. They are designed to move with you, she assured me, and are constructed for comfort in even the most challenging of physical predicaments.

I made sure that I was the only one at home—except for the dogs, of course—when I tried on the sporty unmentionable I'd purchased at a local discount store.

The first thing I noticed is that there were no snaps, Velcro, or hooks. I was expected to slip it on over my head. That exercise took several attempts, with the T-strap giving me a new lesson in physics.

It took me less than 15 seconds to realize I was being choked to death. I'd bought my usual size, but obviously these sports models didn't adhere to traditional sizing.

Now the challenge was to remove the silly thing before it squeezed me as flat as a toothpaste tube. I assumed the standard Female Upper Torso Garment Removal Position: left hand crosses in front of body to grasp lower edge of garment on right side of body; right hand crosses body to grab left hem. Pull up to remove garment over head. That maneuver doesn't always work with fat ladies, and it especially doesn't work when the "hem" is right under your … uh, diaphragm.

Next I tried the male version of garment removal: grab the collar of the garment behind your head, approximately where the label is, and pull it over your head. This device did not have a collar, and my arms were much too short to reach the upper edge of the T-strap running up the center of my back.

I will be forever grateful that our Labrador retriever can neither talk nor operate a video camera.

That way, others will never know the ballet of the bra I choreographed in the privacy of my own home. Neither will they know the words that went with my little dance. I solemnly swear that I have never, ever, called a piece of underwear that particular noun before.

I took a much-deserved break from my gyrations to

have hysterics. I also let the sea breeze coming through the window dry the ladylike glow that had popped up all over my body during the last few minutes.

As my overheated flesh cooled, rational thought returned. It was an inexpensive bra, I reasoned; I could cut it off and no one would ever know. But, I sighed, that would be giving in. I would spend the rest of my life knowing that I had been outsmarted by a wisp of cotton and elastic.

I stood up with renewed determination, grabbed the right armhole (if this bra could claim to have such a thing), and pulled it away from my body to free my arm. A flick of the other wrist and the bra went flying. The Labrador tracked its graceful arc while I had what I hoped would be my last bout of hysterics for the day.

By the time you read this, I will be more or less safely on my way to the upside down part of the world. I have purchased a sports bra that is two sizes larger than what the charts call for, so there shouldn't be any fandangos by Floridians in my Brisbane hotel room.

G'day, mate.

7 May 2004

The Witch of Washington Center

I want it understood right up front that I am not a pilot; the flying wisdom I am about to impart has been carefully reviewed by the chief pilot in my life.

Our latest airborne adventure began a few days after Christmas. Despite my loud protestations about traveling to the Frozen North, Andrew pointed Rudolph the Red-Nosed Cessna toward Virginia and Maryland.

As usual, he had spent the days before our departure on planning our flight; he carefully plotted the course, and then gathered all of the pertinent publications he would need. He was particularly thorough this time, because we would be landing at Manassas Regional Airport, a field we'd never visited.

An added challenge was that this airport is in the Washington, D.C., control area, and he would be talking to Washington Center, one of the nation's busier air traffic control facilities. Washington Center is the big brother to our facility at Hilliard, affectionately known as Jacksonville Center. Jax Center and Washington Center both provide the same service, but Washington has a kabillion more airplanes to worry about. Mr. Curtin worked long and hard to make sure that he and Rudolph would acquit themselves well in this challenging environment. To make things even more demanding, air traffic controllers are serious people in a serious job, and the years since the World Trade Center have made them even more so.

The morning of our departure we stuffed Rudolph with luggage, Christmas presents, and every chart, publication, and check list that any pilot could wish for. Everything went well; Rudolph chugged along, and we ticked off the segments of Andrew's flight plan as we met every milestone. The flight was uneventful until we approached Washington Center; there was more traffic, more chatter on the radio, and that chatter was so fast it sounded like a machine gun. Now I understood why Andy had been so meticulous in his planning.

I have forgotten to explain that someone during the primordial beginnings of American civil aviation drew imaginary highways in the air. It is along these imaginary highways that pilots are directed to fly, especially in bad weather or when the skies are very crowded. As you can imagine, serious deviations from these highways can have serious consequences. I assure you that the Curtins were paying close attention to them as we entered the domain of Washington Center.

Andy introduced himself and our aircraft to the center, and there followed rapid-fire directions: we were to use a Code Four Arrival procedure to reach Manassas Regional. I felt as well as heard Andy's silence at that directive.

"Did she say Code Four Arrival?" he asked.

"That's what I heard," I responded. Andy asked the controller to repeat her directions, which she did—a little faster and a whole lot crankier.

By this time, Andy was flipping through the Instrument Approach Book. "Please say again. I am unfamiliar with the Code Four Arrival."

You know how people can imply that you're an imbecile by their tone of voice? She had polished that act to perfection. "It's in the book; it's been used for years." This circular conversation continued until she crowed that a co-worker had found Code Four on page 5 of the Instrument Approach Book. (It took me two days to realize that even she'd had to look it up!)

We turned to the appropriate page and were appalled. First of all, the arrival wasn't a Code Four; it was COATT-4. That's when I named her the Witch of Washington Center. Thanks, lady, for your help. COATT-4 is a made-up name for a very long and very complicated airborne route through the congested skies of our nation's capital. It makes provisions for stacking aircraft in one of several racetrack holding patterns while they wait to land at one of the many runways in the Washington Center's control area. Rudolph would be playing do-si-do with the commercial airliners (affectionately and accurately called "Big Iron") going into Reagan National and Dulles International airports. Yikes!

I suppressed a whimper as we approached the first navigational aid on this overly challenging pathway; the Witch then announced that we were leaving her fiefdom and would now have to contact Potomac Approach Control.

When Andy told the new controller that we were executing the COATT-4 arrival, there was a slight pause before a very kind voice said, "Oh, no; we're not going to do that to you. Proceed direct to Manassas Regional as filed."

We were safely on the ground in Manassas 30 minutes later. Our Happy Hour was punctuated by a toast to the Witch of Washington Center; I hope her cauldron is always half empty.

22 February 2008

CRITTERS

You Can Bet Your Patootie— Chopped Liver Ain't All That Bad

My husband loudly announced one day that it was time to add canines to the Curtin household. He wanted a black Labrador retriever, for neither yellow nor chocolate would do. And the new puppy would have to be all boy; no girls would be allowed in this club.

I raised my feminazi eyebrows and countered that I would then choose a little girl dog to keep me company and I would find her at the pound. Andy's Rush Limbaugh eyebrows got their own workout, but we shook hands to seal the deal.

During our third or fourth trip to the breeder, we came across a baby black Lab who was standing in his water bowl cooling off his Important Parts. "Smart dog," my husband said. "We'll take that one." I watched from the sidelines as he and his new pup spent days deciding which name to choose.

As he and Bosun were busy bonding, I made yet another trip to the Humane Society in my search for Patootie. I had chosen her name years ago; now all I had to do was to find the dog who fit it. She would be a fluffy dandelion with beady black eyes and a saucy tail.

To make this two-dog family work, we would have to live in what I called the House of Marital Harmony. Andy and Bosun would sit and stay in one side of a duplex, while Patootie and I would reside in the other. Doors would be installed at strategic spots so we could indulge in unfettered visiting. Or not.

Andy and Bosun would furnish their side in Early Yard Sale so they could roll around in the mud and the blood and the beer, to quote some famous dead songwriter. Patootie and I, on the other hand, would sit on velvet cushions, surrounded by antiques and *objets d'art*. We two genteel ladies would listen to classical music while I executed complicated needlework masterpieces.

Fat chance.

The four of us live in an over-remodeled, rambling home where nothing is plumb and a series of half-steps up or down (depending on whether you're coming or going) delineate the limits of each remodeling project attempted by our predecessors. Come over some time and I'll show you the Door to Nowhere.

Bosun was almost housebroken when I finally met Patootie. She was nothing like I envisioned. Instead of a dandelion, I found myself falling in love with a beagle mix. The operative word here is "mix." While she almost looks like a beagle, her temperament and personality led us first to believe her other progenitor might have been a badger or a Tasmanian devil. After 13 years of dithering, we have attributed her sociopathic tendencies to one of the more aggressive terrier types. She is high energy, high maintenance, and high crime. She is also extremely cute, and dons her "cute" face just before we reach out to strangle her.

Unfortunately for us humans, the ten-week-old pups bonded seamlessly the moment they met. Equally unfortunate for us, Patootie elected herself the leader of our four-creature pack. The first example of her leadership was to convince Bosun that housebreaking was an unnecessary annoyance. *Oy*. Instead of my girly-girly dog, I have Osama bin Beagle, who specializes in rolling around in the mud and the blood, and rotting dead things on the beach.

My role in this menagerie is to play the part of Chopped Liver. I sit in my dainty wing chair and turn up the volume on the classical music when the three of them go thundering by, coming from or going to their latest foray into mayhem. Chopped Liver gets up most mornings when Patootie barks. Why can't she bark at Andy at 5:30 in the morning? And Chopped Liver awakes from her after-work nap when Patootie huffs hot breath on her dangling hand.

"We're going to the beach!" The three thunder by as Chopped Liver starts the laundry. And she fetches (you should pardon the expression) the first aid kit when they come back with thorny paws. Chopped Liver sneaks them treats that our Adult Supervision says they cannot have.

But when Chopped Liver gets sick or injured and repairs to the guest room, the Demonic Duo stays with their buddy Andy. One morning, he'll find my cold, dead body only because Patootie is barking at it to get up and fix her breakfast.

Being chopped liver ain't all bad; I get to lie on the sunny spot and cuddle a big hairy dog; I am allowed to scratch the special patch that makes Patootie close her eyes. She and I sometimes share the leftovers while we do the dinner dishes; the boys are in the other room, busy watching football.

Happiness isn't just a warm puppy; it's a puppy who licks the Cool Whip off of the spoon, and then gives your fingers an extra lick that says, "Thanks, Mom."

17 December 2004

Nurse Ratched Is Alive and Well

Someone should have warned me that being on the sick or injured list in the Curtin family is not for sissies.

Our first Labrador retriever turned into Nancy Nurse when either of us two-leggers was incapacitated. There's one famous story about my being in bed for four days with the flu, while Hannibal lay beside me for the duration. We would get up periodically to eat Chicken and Stars soup (his favorite), then make a beeline for bed and a post-lunch nap. When I went back to work, Andy took Hannibal on a forced march to burn all of that canine energy he'd built up during the preceding four days.

It wasn't long after we adopted our current Lab that I began telling everyone that he's really an Irish retriever because he is O'Blivious. In sickness and in health, Bosun snoozes on, unaware of any emergency—medical or otherwise—that might arise. And you can forget his role as a guard dog. We always choose the black Labs because we think they look intimidating to someone contemplating mischief. I hope the erstwhile felons in Fernandina never realize that all you have to do is coo and pat your leg in invitation, and any Labrador will gleefully welcome his newest friend. Now that Bosun is 12 years old, I find myself saying to various service people, "Please don't wake up my guard dog." We chuckle at the black lump as I lead a perfect stranger deeper and deeper into the privacy of our home. Thank goodness this is Fernandina.

Patootie, however, is quite another story. This beagle/Jack Russell(?) mix was my introduction to the Nassau County Humane Society, and I am happy to report that both dog and society are still going strong. While Bosun is comatose most of the time, Patootie is his opposite. There is neither a grasshopper nor a trash truck that escapes her notice or loud comment.

One of the consequences of her rough start in life is that she hates other dogs (except Bosun) and is terrified of people. She bullies Fabio, the harlequin Great Dane she meets on the beach, while Debbie from Kelly Pest Control serviced our account for six months before she ever saw Patootie, the Stealth Dog.

Stealth Dog has recently earned her new nickname of Osama bin Beagle for her various acts of mischief and mayhem around the house. Even at her advanced age (12, by Jim Hicks' estimate), she still steals dirty underwear as I sort laundry; she gathers all of the chew toys and growls at Bosun when he gets too close; and she waits until I am settled with my drink and my book before she demands to go out. This morning she held reveille 15 minutes before the alarm was set to go off by planting two front feet on the bed and barking in my ear.

But when Patootie was younger and thinner (weren't we all?) she would leap onto my sickbed, always landing in the middle of my pain-raddled body. Once safely aboard, she would stomp up and down this body while sniffing it to determine, I presume, whether or not I were still alive. Once satisfied, she would use me as a springboard from which to launch her leap down to the floor. For this wonderful bedside manner, we named her Nurse Ratched, Jack Nicholson's nemesis in "One Flew Over the Cuckoo's Nest."

One quirk of our marriage is that we both require solitude when we are injured or medically challenged. Over the years, we have devised the ritual that the incapacitated partner repairs to the guest room for the duration. It's on another floor at the opposite end from the master bedroom, so there's enough solitude for even a Trappist monk.

My sore hip and I lurked in the guest room for several weeks; at first, I enjoyed the solitude so I could concentrate on being miserable. Jana Diaz had showed me how to place pillows strategically to support my wounded hip, so sleepin' single in a double bed seemed to be the only way to go.

My latest exile to the guest room reminded me to be careful what I ask for. Both O'Blivious and Nurse Ratched stayed with Andrew in the master bedroom; I could have died before morning at the other end of the house and no one would have noticed.

I made that loud observation after a particularly uncomfortable night. Neither dog stopped snarfing down breakfast, and Andrew's expression of sympathy seemed to lack a couple of violins.

It's hard to stomp off in a huff when you walk like a duck.

13 August 2004

This Lizard Queen Rules Supreme!

The Chinese have the Year of the Dog, but the Curtins have done them one better—we have had the Summer of the Lizards.

I must admit that when this Virginia-raised girl first moved to the Sunshine State, I was appalled at the variety, uniqueness, and abundance of Florida's critters. We didn't call them palmetto bugs where I came from, but regardless of the geography, they still made me scream. Mice I could handle, but those big brown babies made me stand on my chair and yell for help. The book exchange on Ash Street introduced me to wood spiders, and I listened to the footsteps of a full-grown adult as it tromped by me late one afternoon. It was as large as the lid on a pint-sized jar of mayonnaise.

But nothing prepared me for what has walked, slithered, and stalked out of the undeveloped lot behind our house: blue tailed skinks I have had to arm-wrestle to get to my car; rattlesnakes toadally enjoying their lunch on our patio; banana spiders in July and our guard bees in the spring. I actually like the bees; they hover about as we do outside chores. Andy and the bees wash our cars on lazy summer afternoons.

The Curtins and their dogs have quite a history with hoppy toads. In Virginia Beach, I discovered our first Labrador retriever cornered by one of these small creatures. The dog was terrified, so I had to overcome my girly-girly squeamishness and scoop up the toad to relocate him. It wasn't pleasant, but it beat explaining to my husband how our Lab died of fright in the back yard.

But nothing prepared me for the large number of hoppy toads in Fernandina. Patootie, our auxiliary dog, used to have great fun pooching them with her nose to make them jump. One day I discovered Patootie with the most peculiar look on her face, so I raced her to Jim Hicks. We never figured out what made her liver go bananas, but she has never again even acknowledged the presence of a hoppy toad.

And now this year, we have lizards, lizards that come in all shapes and sizes and colors. The skinks and I have met before, but now there is a long, skinny, bright green creature whose narrow, elongated snout reminds me of a crocodile. He lives on and near our back gate, and glares at me as I off-load all of the Publix and Wal-Mart bags. If I could glare like that, I could turn people to stone.

The black ones with the yellow stripes enjoy the north side of the house, as do what must be their cousins; their yellow stripes are accented by blue or white dots. Out front, on the eastern side of our house, lives a colony of what I think are chameleons. They change colors as they skitter about, and I am careful to drive slowly down the drive to give them time to reach safety. Only in Paradise does one have time for a lizard parade.

And, oh—I almost forgot to mention the little green geezer with that sexy red bladder under his chin. The first time I saw him, I thought he'd gotten into discarded bubble gum. I don't see him very often, but he does seem partial to our patio table and the shade the umbrella offers. That table is a popular gathering spot, but I seem to be the only one amused at the editorial comments our lizard colony leaves us.

My absolute favorites are the chunky ones who live around our big green garbage can. They have barrel-shaped bodies and a feisty attitude, so I have dubbed them the Jack Russell terriers of the lizard world. I am afraid, however, that their comical bowleg walk somewhat detracts from their fierceness. Their colors range from olive drab on top to pale mustard on their bellies. They have a frill that runs from snout to tail, and when I interrupt them in whatever important business they are conducting, that frill goes rigid as they stop and glare at my impertinence.

I'm afraid I have insulted these downsized dragons, because I cracked up the first time one of them gave me his best glare and came forth with that aggressive pumping, push-up motion. If you don't hear from me for a while, it's probably because one of them dragged me behind the garbage can to have his lizardly way with me.

9 September 2005

Not Your Average Streetwalker

To those of you who wave and honk at me as I schlep my way up and down South Fletcher, thank you—I need all of the encouragement I can get. And if you feel compelled to laugh at my efforts, please turn up your radio so I can't hear you.

The direction I take on South Fletcher is determined by the wind; a head wind on the way back home is bad news. Every walk is an adventure whatever direction I choose, like the other day when I spoke to this nicely dressed woman who was standing on the sidewalk as if she were waiting for a bus. I nodded politely as I passed, and then hid a smile when I heard the familiar *bang*! of the Farmer John; another man had marked his territory. I may miss this parade when the house across the street is finished.

One of the few complaints I have about my trek is the great number of people who park their vehicles on the sidewalk. I try to be patient with the work crews; they're busy earning a living, and they need quick and easy access to the tools and equipment in their trucks. Besides, where else can they park?

I muttered to myself recently as I skirted a lawn service truck, complete with its trailer for hauling mowers, blowers, and whackers. The guys didn't notice me and my mutterings; they were busy doing what they'd been hired to do.

Even the longest walk has a turn-around point, so I was on my way back to the house when one of my latest adventures began to unfold. I saw that the lawn guys were now stowing their equipment, but I also noticed something moving across the street from them. I turned my head to watch as one of the most beautiful Yorkshire terriers I have ever seen ran down the side yard of her house. I knew instantly that she wasn't supposed to be out and about on her own. She made a bee-line for the street, and I knew she wasn't supposed to be there, either.

I also knew I'd never get to her in time, so I sucked in a lungful of air and screamed, "You! Get that dog!" (Even after all of these years of retirement, it was gratifying to know that I could still bark orders with officer-like authority.) One of the guys whirled to discover the Yorkie. By now, she had become frightened at her sudden freedom, and had sat down to think about it—right on the yellow line painted down the middle of South Fletcher. He called softly to her, and she scampered safely into his arms.

I had finally waddled my way to meet them; we were just beginning to wonder what to do with her, when here came her Mamma, running and yelling for her. I carried the Yorkie back to Mamma, who thanked me profusely for saving her dog. I told her that she should really thank the lawn guy for luring her dog out of the street, but he and his coworkers were pulling out with nary a glance our way. I guess saving damsels in distress—regardless of the number of legs they have—was just another day at work for them.

My adventures continued on my next walk. I had just started the home stretch when I spied yet another Yorkie on the loose. This one had to be all boy; his cocky attitude and swagger gave him away. He glared at me as he marched down his driveway to the mailbox and its peemail. I knew that he wasn't supposed to be out without supervision, so I clapped my hands and told him to go back where he belonged. His male bravado evaporated, and he turned tail (literally) and ran back up the driveway. His thank-you was the scowl he shot me for ruining his adventure and damaging his dignity. What is it with Yorkshire terriers, anyway?

My week's adventures culminated when I came upon a box turtle working very hard (and very slowly) to reach the edge of South Fletcher. This creature was not pleased when I turned it around to face the sandy lot with Susan Laird's sign on it. May God rest your soul, Susan, and may that grumpy turtle find a safe home underneath your sign.

My husband has learned to be careful when he asks me about my walk. Heaven only knows what long, drawn-out tale he will hear, but it's sure to involve his wife's encounters with the local flora and fauna.

15 June 2007

All Dogs Go To Heaven

"**I** think God will have prepared everything for our perfect happiness in Heaven. If it takes my dog being there, I believe he'll be there." The Reverend Billy Graham said that, and I certainly hope he is correct.

We returned from an evening of meetings and a late dinner at The Surf to be greeted only by Patootie, our auxiliary dog.

We found Bosun, our 14½-year-old Labrador, in a dark corner of the yard. We helped him into the kitchen, and it was only then that we could see the gravity of the situation.

Andy poured us a nightcap, and we sat at the kitchen table with Bosun at our feet as we sipped good scotch and cried. I don't know who started it, but we began to tell each other funny stories about our dear friend. The beagle part of Patootie chases crabs on the beach, just like a real beagle chases rabbits. Every once in a while, Bosun feels sorry for the crab and scoops it up in that famously gentle Lab mouth. He lifts his head high to keep the crustacean out of Patootie's reach while he carries it to the surf line. When he's ankle deep, he releases it with a most satisfying "plop," and Patootie goes berserk with anger and frustration. I know for a fact that dogs do smile, because Bosun always gets this self-satisfied smirk on his face when he manages to bedevil Patootie.

We told stories late into the night, and the ones about Bosun eventually segued into tales about our first Labrador, Hannibal. We lived in Virginia then, and I remember being mesmerized one summer afternoon as I watched this huge black dog go from bush to bush to sniff the roses. He would ever-so-gently insert his big nose deep into the blossom, and then take a long—and audible—snootful. Everything was fine until he discovered the whiskey barrel full of geraniums. I watched his eyes cross as their peppery scent hit his sensitive schnoz. He was staggering by the time he finished sneezing. Of course, it didn't help matters that I had collapsed in laughter. For all of their gentle ways, Labradors are masters at the dirty look; I found that out the hard way.

We eventually came to the end of both stories and scotch; even our tears had dried up for the moment. We changed into grunge clothes, and I made a pallet on the floor near Bosun so Andy and I could take turns sleeping next to him. My arthritic hips were not too happy with only a fluffy blanket between them and the hard tile floor; when I thought Bosun was safely asleep, I sneaked into the living room to lie on the soft couch. That didn't last long; he soon began to whine for me, so it was back to the pallet. I knew I would hobble around for the next few days, but I really didn't care.

We did not greet the dawn with joy. We moved slowly and quietly through an abbreviated morning routine, and when it was time, we drove to the Amelia Island Animal

Hospital. Jim Hicks and his staff were waiting for us; they have known Bosun all of his life. They took us to one of the private rooms, and we arranged ourselves around the examination table. We'd brought Patootie along so she could say goodbye too, and we put her in a chair so she could see everything that was going on. Just as Doc Hicks removed his stethoscope for the last time, Patootie began to tremble violently, and I knew she understood she'd just lost her best friend. We'd been right to bring her.

We returned home to stumble through the rest of the day. Amelia's Bloomin' Baskets delivered a pot of cheery daisies a couple of hours later, with a card signed by the folks at the hospital. What a class act.

Now it's just the three of us, and I have noticed that we have a tendency to stare off into space from time to time, remembering what it was like when we were four. My knee still automatically moves to nudge Bosun out of the way while I'm working at the kitchen sink, and there's an empty space where he used to lie so he could watch Andy shave every morning. Fortunately, we have a picture of him doing just that and have captioned it "Head in Head."

I like to think that Hannibal is busy teaching Bosun to sniff the roses and to avoid the geraniums while both of them await our arrival. You'd better be right, Reverend Graham.

21 October 2005

There's a New Man in My Life

I have been keeping a secret from you, Gentle Readers. There is a new man in my life I have neglected to tell you about.

Late one February afternoon, the Curtins were driving by the Nassau County Humane Society on Airport Road when we spotted several dog walkers out with their charges. "I want to meet that dog," I said, and pointed to a small black and white dog with large ears.

Our beloved Demonic Duo was long-gone, and our dogless house had grown larger and emptier every day. We had visited Lynda Mixson at RAIN and the litter she'd named after Greek and Roman gods. Apollo was a cute pup, but he was going to grow 50 pounds too large. We went to every Yappy Hour at Falcon's Nest that's hosted by Bark Avenue Pet Boutique, and met several volunteers from STARS and their foster dogs. They were cute, too (the dogs, I mean), but the whistles and bells still did not sound off. I had also become a frequent visitor at the Humane Society; I would pet and hold as many dogs as I could lay my hands on, but I'd always come home empty-handed.

Until I saw Ace that February afternoon. He was 18

pounds of attitude, giving his walker a good workout. He greeted me like a long-lost friend, and I was a goner. We were leaving soon for one of our famous flyabouts, so I presented myself and my checkbook at the Humane Society before we left town to put a deposit on the dog. We spent the entire trip trying to come up with a perfect name for him, but by the time we returned to Paradise, we knew that he already had one.

Ace was waiting for us when we returned, and we now faced the medical challenge the society had warned us about. Ace had a serious case of heartworms. We could foster him during the treatment; if it was successful, we could then adopt him.

Dr. Gilbert at Nassau Veterinary Clinic in Yulee made sure that Ace never realized that he was at the vet's. Instead of placing him on the exam table, she and her tech got down on the floor with him. Lots of treats and one quick shot later, the play date was over. And so it went for several months. We watched him carefully and thought we saw improvement after every date with Dr. Gilbert. Part of his recovery required us to keep him as quiet as possible, but he always went a little crazy at the clinic when he saw Ashley, his fav-o-rite tech in the whole wide world.

Ace was declared heartworm-free this April, and the Curtins promptly adopted him into his forever home. We have watched him as he has grown stronger, healthier, and happier each day.

It didn't take us long to realize that this is a very gregarious dog. He demands to meet and greet everyone we see on our walk. He bestows puppy kisses on the humans within tongue range, and strains at the leash to exchange sniffs with the dogs. Since he is an only dog, at least for now, we grew concerned that he might grow lonely, so it was off to the Humane Society's Dog Park. We have become frequent visitors, and it is rounding out his social life quite nicely. There are separate exercise areas for both large and small dogs; the small dogs can visit the pond and its waterfall, while the larger ones can play in a Milk Bone-shaped pool. Neat, huh? Ace isn't too interested in the water, but he does enjoy a good romp.

I have always been an advocate of animal rescue groups, and this latest adventure has only cemented my high regard for both these organizations and the people who rescue the animals. These tough economic times are proving to be equally tough for these groups. Pets have become luxuries that some families can no longer afford, so the number of turn-ins to our local groups has surged over the past few months.

This surge means that this is an excellent time to find that four-legged friend you've been searching for; everyone I have talked to has an overabundance of critters. This overabundance also means that now is a great time for you to throw a little extra support at your favorite group. Towels, food, toys, treats, and of course money, are always welcome.

Time is always the most valuable commodity that you can volunteer, the one that is always in the shortest supply. And who knows, becoming a foster parent or a dog walker may benefit you just as much as it does the four-legger! I'm sure your own dog would enjoy a play date at the Dog Park—just be sure to look for me and Ace. WOOF!

24 July 2009

About the Author

CARA CURTIN got her B.A. in English and promptly found a job as a copywriter at an advertising agency in Norfolk, Virginia. It took her three years of writing billable copy to discover that she was starving to death. She joined the Navy when the recruiter promised her a living wage. When she completed Officer Training School, the Navy first sent her to Public Affairs School in Indianapolis and then to Pensacola, Florida, as a public affairs officer. She used her writing skills every day of her twenty-year career.

After she retired, Cara opened the Sailor's Wife Book Exchange in Fernandina Beach and began to write about her community. Her by-line appeared regularly in *Amelia Now* and *Amelia Islander Magazine* and she became active in the Nassau County Writers and Poets Society.

She and Foy Maloy, publisher of the *News-Leader*, became the PR committee for the first Book Island Festival, subsequently renamed the Amelia Island Book Festival. It was from that successful collaboration that Cara was invited to write her *City Sidebar* column for the paper. She continues to make her irreverent observations about life in Paradise.

Cara's book writing career began when David Tuttle led the Writers and Poets Society in its project of producing a group novel. *Murder in Fernandina* was an instant success, and soon people were asking for more adventures of Lieutenant Wilson. David wrote the second book, *The Leopard of Fernandina*, and asked Cara to edit it. The Tuttle/Curtin writing team collaborated on the third book in the series, *Fernandina's Lost Island*. As they worked on *Lost Island*, they wondered what would happen next to the intrepid lieutenant. Wilson's next adventure is showcased in *Fernandina's Finest Easter*, and introduces his young protégé Jon Stewart.

Also Read...

Murder in Fernandina

Lieutenant Wilson wants to escape Miami and its high homicide rate, so he takes a job heading the Investigations Division at the Fernandina Beach Police Department. His first day on the job proves to be pure murder, and soon the lieutenant is caught up with treasure maps, a beautiful redhead, and some of the island's more colorful characters. Readers also get a peek into Fernandina history and its notable inns, homes and churches.

The Leopard of Fernandina

Wilson's murderous adventures continue, again woven around the island's rich history. Wilson objects when his new chief volunteers him to be a member of a joint task force, but he finally gets to meet the Man in Green, and it is not love at first sight. The book was written by David Tuttle, lead writer of the first Wilson Mystery, and edited by Cara Curtin.

Fernandina's Lost Island

Co-authors Tuttle and Curtin plotted this third adventure while they were busy working on the lieutenant's second one. This time, Wilson discovers that the bad guys are using the Fernandina Beach Municipal Airport in their skullduggery and Dianne, now a police officer, discovers a new—and risky—interest in pre-Columbian art.

Fernandina's Finest Easter

In the fourth book of the series, authored by Cara Curtin, Sue Nell Borden finds a Labrador puppy on her porch one Easter morning. When the local veterinarian discovers the pup's amazing secret, he realizes it's going to take both him and the dog, as well as some sleuthing by "Fernandina's Finest," to save Sue Nell from a web of danger.

The Pelican of Fernandina *(coming in April 2011)*

Captain Wilson's fifth adventure, begun by the late David Tuttle, is Wilson's most dangerous yet, and it takes the combined efforts of his entire team to extricate him from two sets of bad guys—a fed and a fanatic bent on mass destruction. When Cara Curtin took up the tale, she discovered that the team is distracted from saving its captain by pregnancies, too much local history, and a very important anniversary celebration. To complicate things further, a scary group has taken over one of the town's stately homes. As always, the Pelican watches it all to help when he can—and pick up the pieces when he can't.